Philosophy, Literature and Understanding

Also available from Bloomsbury

Philosophy through Science Fiction Stories, edited by Helen De Cruz, Johan De Smedt and Eric Schwitzgebel
The Aesthetic Illusion in Literature and the Arts, by Tomáš Koblížek
The Cognitive Value of Philosophical Fiction, by Jukka Mikkonen
The Philosophy of Science Fiction, by James Burton

Philosophy, Literature and Understanding

On Reading and Cognition

Jukka Mikkonen

BLOOMSBURY ACADEMIC
LONDON • NEW YORK • OXFORD • NEW DELHI • SYDNEY

BLOOMSBURY ACADEMIC
Bloomsbury Publishing Plc
50 Bedford Square, London, WC1B 3DP, UK
1385 Broadway, New York, NY 10018, USA
29 Earlsfort Terrace, Dublin 2, Ireland

BLOOMSBURY, BLOOMSBURY ACADEMIC and the Diana logo
are trademarks of Bloomsbury Publishing Plc

First published in Great Britain 2021
This paperback edition published in 2022

Copyright © Jukka Mikkonen, 2021

Jukka Mikkonen has asserted his right under the Copyright,
Designs and Patents Act, 1988, to be identified as Author of this work.

For legal purposes the Acknowledgements on p. viii constitute an
extension of this copyright page.

Cover image: *The Reader in the Forest*, Robert Henri, 1918,
Museum of Fine Arts, Houston, US.

All rights reserved. No part of this publication may be reproduced or
transmitted in any form or by any means, electronic or mechanical, including
photocopying, recording, or any information storage or retrieval system,
without prior permission in writing from the publishers.

Bloomsbury Publishing Plc does not have any control over, or responsibility for,
any third-party websites referred to or in this book. All internet addresses given
in this book were correct at the time of going to press. The author and publisher
regret any inconvenience caused if addresses have changed or sites have ceased
to exist, but can accept no responsibility for any such changes.

A catalogue record for this book is available from the British Library.

Library of Congress Cataloging-in-Publication Data

Names: Mikkonen, Jukka, author.
Title: Philosophy, literature and understanding: on
reading and cognition / Jukka Mikkonen.
Description: London; New York: Bloomsbury Academic, 2021. |
Includes bibliographical references and index. |
Identifiers: LCCN 2020049933 (print) | LCCN 2020049934 (ebook) |
ISBN 9781350163966 (hardback) | ISBN 9781350163973 (ebook) |
ISBN 9781350163980 (epub)
Subjects: LCSH: Fiction–Psychological aspects. | Psychology and
literature. | Narration (Rhetoric) | Cognition.
Classification: LCC PN3352.P7 M55 2021 (print) |
LCC PN3352.P7 (ebook) | DDC 808.3–dc23
LC record available at https://lccn.loc.gov/2020049933
LC ebook record available at https://lccn.loc.gov/2020049934

ISBN: HB: 978-1-3501-6396-6
PB: 978-1-3502-2901-3
ePDF: 978-1-3501-6397-3
eBook: 978-1-3501-6398-0

Typeset by Deanta Global Publishing Services, Chennai, India

To find out more about our authors and books visit
www.bloomsbury.com and sign up for our newsletters.

To Kerttu, Pieti and Veini

Contents

Acknowledgements   viii

1 Introduction   1
2 Imagination   13
3 Narrative   41
4 Cognition   59
5 Evidence   89

Notes   119
References   153
Index   178

Acknowledgements

This book is based on work carried out in several research projects on art and cognition from 2011 onward. During these years, I have had the opportunity to work with wonderful people from whom I have learnt a lot. First of all, I want to thank the members of the *Cognitive Relevance of Aesthetics* group, Hanne Appelqvist and Kalle Puolakka, for years of fruitful collaboration. I have also had an opportunity to work with narrative scholars in the *Dangers of Narrative* group and the *Instrumental Narratives* research consortium, for which I am grateful. In particular, I want to thank Maria Mäkelä, Merja Polvinen, Hanna Meretoja, Samuli Björninen, Laura Karttunen, Johanna Kaakinen and Matti Hyvärinen. For comments, cooperation and correspondence I want to express my gratitude to Leila Haaparanta, Sami Pihlström, Arto Haapala, Peter Lamarque, Stein Haugom Olsen, Gregory Currie, Catherine Z. Elgin, John Gibson, Wolfgang Huemer, Tzachi Zamir, Eileen John, Derek Matravers, Stacie Friend, Elisabeth Schellekens, Bo Pettersson, Alberto Voltolini, Garry Hagberg, Marya Schechtman, Patrik Engisch and Julia Langkau. I also want to thank my colleagues in Philosophy in Tampere and the philosophical *niin & näin* magazine collective. Finally, I am grateful for Dr Tommi Kakko for proofreading the manuscript and for an anonymous referee for his or her invaluable comments.

The studies which this work is based on have been funded by various projects and foundations. I want to express my deepest gratitude to the Academy of Finland (Judgment and Human Rationality project, led by Leila Haaparanta, and Instrumental Narratives: The Limits of Storytelling and New Story-Critical Narrative Theory (no. 314768), led by Maria Mäkelä), the Finnish Cultural Foundation (the Cognitive Relevance of Aesthetics project), the Alfred Kordelin Foundation, the Emil Aaltonen Foundation and the Ella and Georg Ehrnrooth Foundation.

A large amount of the book is based on earlier publications that have been extended and revised. I want to thank the publishers for permission to reuse the material in this book. The publications are 'Analytic Philosophy of Literature' in *The Cambridge Handbook of Philosophy of Language*, edited by Piotr Stalmaszczyk (2021); 'On the Cognitive Value of Modernist Narratives' in *The Fictional Minds of Modernism: Narrative Cognition from Henry James to Christopher Isherwood*, edited by Ricardo Miguel Alfonso (2019); 'The (Literary) Stories of Our Lives' in *Narrative and Self-Understanding: Between Literature and Philosophy*, edited by Garry L. Hagberg (2019); 'Truth in Literature: The Problem of Knowledge and Insight Gained from Fiction' in *Narrative Factuality: A Handbook*, edited by Monika Fludernik and Marie-Laure Ryan (2018); 'Analytic Aesthetics' in *Palgrave Handbook of Philosophy and Literature*, edited by Michael Mack and Barry Stocker (2018); 'Analytic Philosophy of Literature: Problems and Prospects' in *Literary Studies and the Philosophy of Literature: New Interdisciplinary Directions*, edited by Phil Gaydon and Andrea Selleri (2016); 'On Studying the Cognitive Value of Literature', *The Journal of Aesthetics and Art Criticism*, Vol. 73, No. 3 (2015); 'The Place for External Considerations in Reading Literary Fiction' in *How to Make-Believe: The Fictional Truths of the Representational Arts*, edited by Alexander Bareis and Lene Nordrum (2015); and 'Fiction, Cognition, and Confusion' in *Fiction and Art: Explorations in Contemporary Theory*, edited by Ananta Ch. Sukla (2015).

1

Introduction

Philosophers have traditionally taken a great interest in the cognitive value of literature, understood as its ability to convey knowledge and insight or to contribute to our understanding of ourselves, others and reality. Initially, the study underlying this book began with age-old academic philosophical questions, such as: *Can works of literature improve the understanding of readers?* and *How is this improvement best conceived of from an epistemological point of view?* However, it suddenly became apparent that 'cognition' and 'benefit' were everywhere, and the question of literature's contribution to readers' thought – namely, social cognition and empathy – had not only become of transdisciplinary interest but also received much popular attention because of bold empirical studies on the topic. This turned my interest towards the reasons why people read, the values sought from literature and methodological issues in the study of art and cognition.

Recently, there has been much interest in art's cognitive and affective impact in psychology and neurosciences.[1] Broadly speaking, the psychological and neuroscientific study of art's improvement of cognition stems from a hectic, individualist, instrumentalist culture where temporary employment and continuous competition are the norms. One has to constantly develop oneself, and office workers need to keep their most valuable instrument, their brains, fit. As Svend

Brinkmann, a psychologist feeling aversion for the 'self-improvement craze', puts it,

> The religion of the self has taken over many of the functions of Christianity: the role of the priest is now played by a psychotherapist or coach; religious denominations have given way to therapy, coaching and other techniques for personal development; grace and salvation have been replaced by self-realisation, skills enhancement and lifelong learning. And finally, perhaps most importantly, where God used to be at the centre of the universe, now it is the self. Never before in history have we talked so much about the self and its characteristics (self-esteem, self-confidence, self-development, etc.). Never before have we had so many ways to measure, evaluate and develop the self – even though we basically have no idea what it is.[2]

What about literature? Frank Hakemulder and his colleagues in the psychology of literature, for example, propose that 'in the contemporary economy it has become more important for workers to be creative, innovative and to have interpersonal skills, and all of these may be influenced through fiction reading'.[3] P. Matthijs Bal and his colleagues, in turn, suggest that empathic skills and enhanced prosociality gained by reading fictional literature could lead to *higher performance, productivity* and *creativity* in the workplace.[4] Further, they suggest that fictional narratives also help workers to *recover*.[5]

In media, fiction is offered as a miracle cure for everything. It is common to see headlines such as 'Reading Literature Makes Us Smarter and Nicer',[6] 'Reading Literary Fiction Can Lead to Better Decision-Making, Study Finds',[7] 'For Better Social Skills, Scientists Recommend a Little Chekhov',[8] 'Novel Finding: Reading Literary Fiction Improves Empathy',[9] 'Want To Read Others' Thoughts? Try Reading Literary Fiction',[10] 'Reading Fiction May Enhance Social Skills',[11] 'Now We Have Proof Reading Literary Fiction Makes You a Better Person',[12] '9 Ways Reading Fiction Will Make You Happier and More Successful',[13] '4 Ways Fiction Makes You a Better Human'[14], 'Five Ways Reading Can Improve Health and Well-Being',[15] 'How Reading Rewires Your Brain for Greater Intelligence and Empathy',[16] 'Why Readers Are Generally More Thoughtful People, According to Science',[17] 'How Reading Increases Your Emotional Intelligence & Brain Function: The Findings of Recent Scientific Studies',[18] 'Reading Fiction Improves Brain Connectivity and Function'[19] or, symptomatic of our time: 'Science Shows Something Surprising About People *Who Still Read Fiction*'.[20]

Few 'can' afford – have the courage to engage in – slow narrative arts today, for the demand of continuous self-improvement is everywhere. When it comes to leisure, there are interesting things all around and not enough hours in the day to explore them. An exhausted student or worker might find it difficult to fight against the temptations of digital media – instant pleasure only one click away. A novel feels heavy in one's hands and the interface of a book obsolete. Digital media also offer *aesthetic* pleasures, equally only a click away, and in terms of *effort* and *payoff*, literary narratives do not seem to fare well. This book examines a part of the distinctive value of literature, although it maintains that the 'cognitive benefits' of literature, if we are to crudely call them that, are not instant and straightforward. Moreover, if literature has real value in affecting one's view of the world, it might rather show one the absurdity of life in late capitalism and help one quit a meaningless job than become a little more friendly at the workplace.

* * *

There are several reasons why the question of the cognitive value of literature has returned to literary studies where it used to be considered a mundane matter. In the 2000s and 2010s, there has been a boom among literary scholars to articulate the values of literature and the study of it.[21] Partly, this is due to the 'crisis' of the humanities and the closing of literature departments. In a utilitarian age, every discipline has had to legitimize itself, and many defenders of literature have preferred to use a language understood by the people in charge and to impress them with buzzwords, such as 'cognition'. As said, literature has also been considered threatened and its role in society weak. Statistics tell us that people, especially young people, spend less and less time 'reading books' which typically means long narratives printed on paper. In these defences, literature is seen, for example, as a way of helping one to understand oneself better or providing places to examine fundamental questions about life and to give meaning to events in one's life; literary works give insights into others' lives and improve the reader's empathic attitude; works of literature celebrate a multiplicity of meaning, perspectives and values; they encourage the reader to look at the world from new viewpoints or to sketch reality anew; and of course, literary works give the reader new worlds to explore and provide distinctive emotional, cognitive, aesthetic and even mystical pleasures.

Another reason for the interest in cognition in the humanities relates to the rise of cognitive science in the 1990s. The sciences of the mind, the top science in the age of the brain, have been interested in the reception of art, and the psychology of art is living its heyday. Literary scholars have either sided with approaches in the cognitive sciences[22] or defended literature's distinctive value from them. There is also a third reason, happily a positive one. Today, literature is again allowed to speak about the world and the reader to reflect its content in relation to reality (after all, literature is not distinct from the world). Minorities have found literature as a medium for exploring, articulating and communicating their experiences,[23] and conversely critical practices – postcolonialism, feminism, posthumanism, for instance – have explored literary works for their political, societal, moral and philosophical import.

***

Philosophical defences of literature's epistemic value have a long history, and they can be, somewhat crudely, reduced back to Aristotle. While the question has puzzled philosophers in virtually all traditions, there has been a special interest in it in analytic philosophy, an approach that has been keen on matters concerning truth and meaning. (Arguably, analytical philosophical problems regarding the epistemology of art are partly self-inflicted and have arisen as the result of philosophers conceiving of knowledge in a frame of comparative narrowness.)

Much of analytic discussion on the cognitive value of art operates on an Arnoldian humanistic conception of literature,[24] in which quality literature is distinguished by its high truth and seriousness. Often, the traditional humanist conception is simply assumed, but recently it has also been philosophically defended. John Gibson, for one, characterizes the humanist view as the thought that 'literature presents the reader with an intimate and intellectually significant engagement with social and cultural reality'.[25] In his view, 'literature is the textual form to which we turn when we want to read the story of our shared form of life: our moral and emotional, social and sexual – and so on for whatever aspects of life we think literature brings to view – *ways of being human*.'[26] Alan Goldman goes on to argue that 'the evaluation of thematic theses uncovered in the process of interpreting, and the learning that occurs in that process of evaluation, are part of the cognitive engagement that is part of the appreciation of the literary value of novels [that contain profound themes]'.[27] For him, 'reflective cognitive exercise', in which the reader evaluates a literary theme for truth or plausibility, is part of the aesthetics appreciation of the work.[28] Richard Gaskin, for his part, argues for 'literary humanism' which maintains that works of literature 'bear on the world' by employing terms that refer to real, principally universal entities, and by making or implying true or false, principally general statements about the world; further, the view holds that some works of literature have cognitive value in that they make or imply true statements that can be known to be true and are worth knowing.[29] Bernard Harrison, in turn, renders 'humanistic literary criticism', a conception promoted by Lionel Trilling, F. R. Leavis, Northrop Frye and M. H. Abrams, as a view that 'took it for granted that major creative literature constitutes one of our main resources for critical reflection on the human condition, both individual and cultural'.[30] In the humanistic conception, '[l]iterary fiction [...] works by deploying words against a background of imagined circumstances in such a way as to allow us to focus on the roots in social practice, with all of its inherent ambiguities and stresses, of the meanings through which we are accustomed to represent our world and ourselves.'[31] Harrison, defending the humanist view, writes: 'If the humanities, including the study of literature, are to be defended as an important part of university studies, then it needs to be shown that they contribute kinds of understanding of the human condition that are different from, and independent of, those contributed by the social sciences.'[32] Finally, Tzachi Zamir maintains that '[e]xceptional literary creations owe much of their value to the relationship between the insights they enable and the experiential pathways via which these insights are reached'.[33]

* * *

But what are 'cognition' and 'cognitive value'? Although 'cognition' in the general scientific sense refers to a wide variety of mental processes from language comprehension to problem-solving, in analytic philosophy of literature it has been customarily identified with 'higher mental states', in particular with the communication of knowledge and acquisition of true beliefs, cognitive value thus being *epistemic* value rather narrowly construed.[34] In different times, however, philosophers have prioritized different kinds of knowledge that the arts could provide. Now in the age of multiculturalism and pluralism, the chief cognitive virtue is not to master universal truths (for there are few of these in domains such as ethics) but to be able to read other people, to understand different viewpoints, to put oneself in another's shoes.

On the other hand, 'cognition' is on the move, and many philosophers have recently been eager to broaden its scope above, or rather below, higher mental states. For instance, in the 4E model cognition is *embodied, embedded, enactive* and *extended*; it gets its shape and structure from the brain, body and physical and social environments. As the literary critic Terence Cave puts it,

> [M]ost cognitivists nowadays give the word 'cognition' a much broader sense, embracing mental functioning and mental processes as a connected whole. Those processes include abstract and rational thought, imagination, emotion, *and somatic reflexes and responses*. These are assumed to be connected and mutually interactive processes.[35]

Today, it seems, the relevant question is What does cognition *not* include and what does *not* improve cognition?[36] A related question is, of course, why literature should have cognitive value, however understood; could it not be serious and valuable without improving the reader's mental functioning? Another important question is whether all cognition is conscious and reflective. Regarding the omnipresence of narratives in our culture and the workings of the human mind, it is likely that artistic and non-artistic narratives affect us much without us noticing it. Should cognitivism, then, attempt to account for the assumed 'unreflective' changes in the reader?[37] This study focuses on the role of literary narratives in one's cultural and self-understanding. It acknowledges that narratives may change us in ways that we do not notice and that what we think we have 'learnt' from literature might differ from what we have actually 'learnt' from them (are not the self and free will fictions, too?). However, it attempts to locate literature in a cultural practice in which we reflect on and discuss the works and how they affect our lives.

* * *

In the history of philosophy, *walking* has been given a high intellectual value.[38] Many great minds would not have prospered without taking to their feet. A great many thinkers have also found profound inspiration in *gardening*. Everyday *conversations* may radically transform one's thinking. Cognition is being enhanced everywhere, all the time. What is special about literature, then? This study maintains that literature has distinctive cognitive value which is based on literary features on the one hand and distinctive imaginative engagement with the work on the other. It also holds that we should not think of reading as an isolated and individual process, an individual psychological phenomenon, but something that takes place within the literary practice and includes critical discourse and collective metacognition.

Literary works may have explicit informative or other 'cognitive' aims, which may be acknowledged or ignored in reading. Moreover, the works may lose these functions in the course of time.[39] Conversely, a literary work may retrospectively acquire psychological, political or social import, for instance. There are also different 'cognitive' ways of approaching works of literature from 'retrieval' (intentionalist interpretation, for example) to 'creative interpretation' (deconstructionist interpretation, for example). Thinking of the heterogeneity of literature and its extensive history, it is doubtful whether a theory of the cognitive value of literature could be both extensive and non-trivial.[40] Moreover, as different literary genres have different epistemological underpinnings, a sophisticated cognitive theory might be expected to be genre-relative.[41] Perhaps, indeed, we should think of literature pluralistically as a 'botanical garden full of many beautiful species, each species implicitly bearing standard of excellence within its kind', as Wayne C. Booth proposes.[42] While I, as a professional philosopher, sketch out general conceptual models related to our imaginative engagement with narrative fictions, I am not, however, so silly as to claim that these would cover all cognition nor all literature.

* * *

The book consists of four chapters which defend literature's cognitive value in terms of understanding and which may be read autonomously. Chapter 2, 'Imagination', offers a view of literary imagining that pays attention to the reader's 'external reflections' in literary experience. In exploring the reader's active role in literary interpretation, I will criticize unduly sharp distinctions typically drawn between either 'imagination' and 'fantasy' or 'interpretation' and the 'use' of a work, showing that the reader's imaginative supplementation of a work's content and her reflection on that content admit a rich dialogue between the work and the world.

In 'Narrative', I will defend the epistemic significance of narratives, everyday and literary. I argue that the recent philosophical attack on the value of narratives operates on problematic concepts and propose that the epistemic significance of narratives is not to be explained in terms of knowledge but understanding. Further, I will explore the value of literary narratives and their potential to contribute to our understanding of ourselves and reality in terms of *processuality* and *artificiality*. I argue that literary works provide their readers insights into the processual dimension of emotions, such as the causes and stages of grief and sorrow, and the unfolding of actions like punishment or forgiving. On the other hand, when readers explore literary narratives from an 'external' viewpoint, acknowledging their artificiality, they gain insight into literary schemes and techniques of storytelling. Such acuity helps them to observe and disentangle the mythical and rhetorical aspects in the stories that surround them and affect their values and behaviour: political speeches, advertisements, entertainment and the like.

A large part of the book concerns the nature of aesthetic cognition. In 'Cognition', I argue that the concept of understanding outperforms the concept of knowledge in its ability to capture the various cognitive values of literary narratives. Nevertheless, this book shows that the enhancement of understanding is not a straightforward process. I will argue that many literary works tend to challenge their readers' conceptions, provoke conceptual explorations and prompt questions but withhold answers, thus triggering thought-processes that might lead the reader to examine and revise her intuitive conceptions. Moreover, I will show how the notion of understanding transforms the debate concerning literature and cognition. The notion of understanding implies, for example, that a fiction's epistemic effect depends partly on the background it operates against, which makes the cognitive benefits of literature relative to the reader (i.e. relational but not relativistic).

While the cognitive function of literature has been extensively theorized in philosophy, little has been said about the effects which literary works actually have on their readers. In 'Evidence', I will investigate the study of learning from literature, its methods and conceptions of evidence, and build bridges between analytic philosophy, literary studies and cognitive psychology in order to gain a broad understanding of the sort of things readers learn (or believe they learn) from literature. I will explore two popular approaches in philosophical aesthetics – the traditional 'armchair' approach which focuses on intuitions and conceptual arguments and the naturalist approach which relies on the sciences – and argue that neither of these approaches is sufficient to support views on literature's epistemic value. Instead, I propose that the place to look for evidence for the cognitive benefits of literature, the reader's enhanced understanding, is the practice of literature and the study of it. I will illustrate the cognitive gains of literature with reference to academic critical analysis (literary interpretation as conducted by professional readers) and literary reception studies (actual responses of the reading public). Besides these two sources of evidence, or aspects of it, I will seek support for the cognitivist's thesis from readers' descriptions of their literary experiences. In particular, I will look at non-fictional writings that traditionally link to literature and emphasize their writers' influences and attitudes to life: essay and autobiography. I examine this sort of testimony as evidence and investigate how readers demonstrate the growth of their understanding.

* * *

In my previous monograph *The Cognitive Value of Philosophical Fiction* (2013), I attempted to tackle the value of explicitly philosophical fictions in terms of propositional knowledge. *L'enfer est plein de bonnes volontés ou désirs.* Such a defence will fail in two ways: on the one hand, it will not change sceptical philosopher's opinion about the significance of literature; on the other hand, literary scholars and the *aficionadi* will not see anything but instrumentalization of art in it. While this book negates my previous work in many ways, it has the same optimistic ethos, and the following chapters are best seen as exercises in futility.

2

Imagination

It is a commonplace that in reading fiction we are immersed in another world and walking in another's shoes. In philosophical aesthetics the paradigmatic view maintains, roughly put, that an engagement with a fiction is about the reader *pretending* or *making-believe* that the story is a true account of events, experiences and the like. This view of the 'fictive stance', the idea of a textually (or authorially) guided immersion, differs from a popular (pretheoretical) conception of *aesthetic experience* in which the imagination is free to move, to make connections between the concrete and the abstract, to associate and mix concepts and ideas and so on. Indeed, analytic philosophers have been keen to set limits for imagination in their theories of fiction. They regularly draw a distinction between *imagination* and *fantasy*, maintaining that in our engagement with works of fiction some imaginings are *appropriate* while some others are not. These limits for the imagination are set in theories of fiction; when philosophers explore literary interpretation, imagination is allowed a more active role, for example, in connecting the particularities of the work with universal themes. Even so, in philosophical theories of literary interpretation, the idea of appropriateness is present as a distinction between the *interpretation* and *use* of a work.

This chapter attempts to make room for different kinds of imaginative activity in literary experience. The first part explores the freedom and limits of imagination in literary experience, the idea of 'appropriate' imagining in reading fictional literature and the characteristics of literary imagination. The latter part argues, *contra* the paradigmatic view, that imaginative engagement with a work of literary fiction commonly involves, and sometimes arguably necessitates, readers reflecting on the fictional content in different ways in relation to reality.

Imagination bound

The study of imagination is divided into various subfields in the contemporary philosophy of literature. Popular topics include, for example, modes of imagining involved in reading fiction (*de se, de re, de dicto*), the role of empathy in literary experience, the nature of emotions that occur in literary imagining and the cognitive impact of literary imagining. However, especially in the analytic tradition, literary imagination has been primarily explored as a propositional attitude – that is, as a mental state which readers adopt towards the content of a literary work.[1] Philosophers have considered imagination in our engagement with fiction mostly propositional, maintaining that reading is about pretending, imagining or making-believe *that* something is the case; moreover, they have associated fictional worlds with fictional propositions. J. L. Austin and John R. Searle famously advocated the idea of fiction-writing and, respectively, literary imagining as 'pretence'.[2] Later, Nicholas Wolterstorff introduced the concept of the 'fictive stance' which 'consists of [the author] *presenting*, or *offering for consideration*, certain states of affairs – for us to reflect on, to ponder over, to explore the implications of, to conduct strandwise extrapolation on'.[3]

The basic elements for contemporary theories of fiction were formed in Kendall Walton's magnum opus on 'make-believe' and Gregory Currie's study of the 'fictive utterance', both published in 1990.

Walton's and Currie's theories have been labelled together as the 'report model' of fiction, although their views differ in various important respects.[4] The model maintains, roughly put, that a reader imagines or makes-believe of the fictional text that she is reading a report of actual events (as reported by someone).[5] Important in Walton's and Currie's views is the idea of prompted or invited imaginings: Walton maintains that fictions *mandate* certain imaginings,[6] whereas Currie states that the author *intends* that readers make-believe the content of the work (partly) as a result of recognizing the author's intention to do so.[7]

While imagination is in everyday parlance generally considered a constructive and creative enterprise, in philosophical theories of fiction it is regularly seen as more of a passive response. Pretence or make-believe is about temporarily adopting (or entertaining) certain beliefs and emotions. But perhaps this is what *reading* is all about? Schopenhauer famously said that '[w]hen we read, someone else thinks for us; we repeat merely his mental process'.[8] While this remark can be seen as a scornful critique of intellectual authorities – scholars who have 'read themselves stupid'[9] – rather than as a genuine description of the act of reading, there has been wide and serious philosophical (and psychological) support for the idea of one's adopting another's mind in reading. For example, the critic Georges Poulet found it astonishing that in reading he is thinking the thoughts of another as his very own – that it is really Baudelaire or Racine who thinks or feels in him.[10] Poulet proposes that

> Reading [. . .] is the act in which the subjective principle which I call *I*, is modified in such a way that I no longer have the right, strictly speaking, to consider it as my *I*. I am on loan to another, and this other thinks, feels, suffers, and acts within me. [. . .] When I am absorbed in reading, a second self takes over, a self which thinks and feels for me.[11]

Even the reception theorist Wolfgang Iser, who considers literary interpretation a dynamic process between the work and the reader, thinks that 'we must suspend the ideas and attitudes that shape our own personality before we can experience the unfamiliar world of the literary text'.[12] The phenomenon must be familiar for everyone. Literary works capture our minds by offering us thoughts together with viewpoints or attitudes concerning those thoughts. This is characteristic for literature, and an attention to the narrative viewpoint a central part of literary response. But one's imaginative engagement is not limited to fiction. In focusing on *narrative* fictions, philosophers have paid relatively little attention to the fact that non-fictional narratives also prompt imaginings. Imagination and immersion occur in our engagements with various kinds of texts, and one may disappear into various sorts of narratives.

> In endless space countless luminous spheres, round each of which some dozen smaller illuminated ones revolve, hot at the core and covered over with a hard cold crust; on this crust a mouldy film has produced living and knowing beings: this is empirical truth, the real, the world. Yet for a being who thinks, it is a precarious position to stand on one of these numberless spheres freely floating in boundless space, without knowing whence or whither, and to be only one of innumerable similar beings that throng press, and toil, restlessly and rapidly arising and passing away in beginningless and endless time. Here there is nothing permanent but matter alone, and the recurrence of the same varied organic forms by means of certain ways and channels that inevitably exist as they do.[13]

While it can be debated whether that passage, the opening of Schopenhauer's *The World as Will and Representation* (1818/1844), is its author's earnest assertion of reality and whether there is much narrativity in it (and while we ought to remember that there may be fictional passages within non-fictions[14]), the passage illustrates that imaginings are not limited to works such as novels.

Moreover, there are different imaginings involved in our encounters with non-fictional works. Some of the imaginings are accidental. For example, I may spontaneously project a sensory image of the proceeding of the Spartan army heading towards its enemy from a laconic report of a historical battle. Some imaginings are, in turn, deliberate and prompted by the text, as in Peter Englund's historical work *The Beauty and the Sorrow: An Intimate History of the First World War* (2011), based on diary accounts, letters, memoirs and other first-hand material:

> Elfriede hears her brother shouting and then she sees it for herself. Here they come, row upon row of soldiers in grey uniforms, short boots of pale, untanned leather, huge knapsacks and pickelhaubes with grey cloth covers. A military band is marching in front and as they approach the great crowd of people at the station they strike up the tune that everyone knows so well.[15]

Is there a difference in the workings of imagination in our responses to fiction and non-fiction? In his *Nature of Fiction* (1990), Currie proposes that a work of history or a newspaper article can 'stimulate the imagination' the same way a fiction does.[16] Nonetheless, he thinks that the reading of fiction differs from the reading of non-fiction, not because of the *activity* of the imagination but because of the *attitude* we adopt towards the content of the work: make-belief in fiction, belief in non-fiction.[17] Over twenty years later, Currie is dissatisfied with the distinction by attitude. Drawing on another distinction between propositional and perceptual imagination, and the idea of the intensity of imagining, he says that 'imaginings vary a good deal in their perceptual and emotional intensity' and that 'it is plausible to suppose that our judgments about the fictional status of a work depend partly on the intensity of the imaginings they provoke'.[18]

There are two peculiar things around the study of fiction and imagination in contemporary aesthetics. First, it seems too restrictive for an aesthetic experience that there is an 'appropriate' imaginative response towards a work, namely, the one mandated by the work or intended by the author. It implies that there is *a certain correct* way to engage with the work. Very few would be happy with this, because much of our interest in artworks relate to their complexity and ambiguity. Second, it seems strange that there would be nothing obviously *distinctive* in imaginatively engaging with a literary-fictional narrative compared to the reading of non-fictional narratives, such as a newspaper article or a work of history. Are there no differences between the kinds of attention the different kinds of works call for?

In analytic aesthetics, philosophers have been generally more interested in the 'fictional' than the 'aesthetic' in literature. This is partly because *fictionality* is an interesting topic from the perspective of many analytical philosophical fields, such as ontology and the philosophy of language.[19] The emphasis on propositional attitudes, together with a focus on realist representation in literature, has dominated the study of imagination. Elisabeth Camp suspects that philosophers have been interested in fiction 'because it seems, at least *prima facie*, to employ the imagination in a way that conforms to a standard model of the mind', namely, mental pretence that comes in two main forms: propositional supposition and experiential imagining.[20] Relatively little has been said of imagination with regard to literary *art*. The role which imagination is given in contemporary aesthetics is impoverished compared to that which it has had before, particularly in its heyday in German romanticism. Even more, the feebleness of literary imagination in contemporary aesthetics is underlined by the interest in 'imaginative resistance', our *inability* or *unwillingness* to imagine certain sort of fictional depictions, such as logical inconsistencies (inability) and immoral views or viewpoints (unwillingness) – a phenomenon of which David Hume, however, was allegedly already familiar. In what follows, I shall explore the limits philosophers have set for imagination in the act of reading, followed by the 'aesthetics' of imagination.

Imagination unbound

There are various sorts of imagining present in our encounters with literary works. To begin with, there are different kinds of imagination associated with different literary historical periods and genres.[21] Further, different modes of imagination might be employed, or foregrounded, in reading prose fiction, drama and lyric poetry. Whereas prose fiction, for instance, characteristically invites narrative (or causal) imagining, lyric poetry is believed to emphasize 'a metaphorical, conceptual transfiguration of actuality'.[22] There are also differences within these broad genres. Tolstoy's realistic novels call for visual imagination and emotional engagement, whereas Borges's essayistic short stories offer thought-experiments difficult to visualize, sometimes even conceive. Adopting someone's point of view or identifying with a character – the commonplace of being in another's shoes – might not be necessary for a 'proper understanding' of a work of fiction. And then there are works which mix various literary forms and thus also kinds of imagining.

Clearly, literary imagination is not limited to the 'reconstruction' of the (textual) meaning of the work. Whereas the analytic tradition has paid much attention to propositional attitudes and fictional propositions, the phenomenological tradition has been interested, among other things, in the reader's act of imaginatively supplementing the fictive utterance. Phenomenological theories of literature and reader-response theories of literary reception have emphasized the reader's role in complementing or 'concretizing' a literary work. The theories maintain that the reader's task is to fill in the gaps, or places of indeterminacy or holes or *lacunae*, in the narrative. A glance at two classics is in order.

In his pioneering work on the philosophy of literary experience, Roman Ingarden speaks of 'places of indeterminacy' (*Unbestimmtheitsstellen*) in a literary text. By the term, he means aspects of the work which are not determined in the text, many of these relating to 'descriptions of what happens to people and things'.[23] Ingarden remarks that places of indeterminacy vary in their significance: some are superficial, whereas some may 'reveal depths in a character, intensify or resolve conflict within him, etc.'[24] Further, Ingarden thinks that much of this 'filling in' is unconscious.[25] He asserts that the reader's act of imaginative supplementation derives from a 'natural inclination', for we are accustomed to think of persons and things as completely determinate.[26] As the places of indeterminacy can be filled in various ways, it follows that the literary work may have considerably different and mutually exclusive 'concretizations'.[27] Different concretizations also emerge because readers differ in their imaginative and critical skills:

> The effectiveness of the aesthetic experience depends primarily on the abilities of the reader, his interest in certain artistic themes, the type of imagination he possesses, the scope and activity of his imagination, the subtlety of his sensitivity, the level of activity of his emotional reaction, the type of aesthetic culture he possesses, and so on.[28]

Similarly, Wolfgang Iser thinks that the kingdom of literary imagination lies in the gaps. He claims that 'without the elements of indeterminacy, the gaps in the text, we should not be able to use our imagination':[29] should texts possess only a meaning to be recovered by a reader, there would be very little to do for literary interpretation.[30] Moreover, Iser claims that no individual reading can ever 'exhaust the full potential' of a literary work as each individual reading fills in the gaps in the narrative in a certain way and thereby excludes various other possibilities.[31]

Several important points can be drawn from these brief paraphrases. First, the significance of indeterminacy in narrative. In order to be interesting, a literary work has to have suitable kinds of gaps in proper places. If the work lacks gaps, it is dull and boring; if it contains too many or too large gaps, it is unexciting, obscure or pretentious.[32] Second, gaps are filled both consciously and unconsciously. We may, and assumedly do, imagine the look of a fictional character without thinking about the matter too much, whereas sometimes we need to think very hard to make the story intelligible. Third, we fill in gaps differently on different readings, and we return to (great) works of literature partly because they yield different 'concretizations' on every reading.[33]

In reading fiction, we follow the story, the storyteller's account, constantly supplementing what is left unsaid, recalling past and anticipating future events. We evaluate the narrator and make inferences about her, doubting her account in cases where she (or the whole narrative) seems unreliable. At the level of the story, we make interpretations of events, heading to the direction that looks most promising. In his *Six Walks in the Fictional Woods* (1994), Umberto Eco compares a work of fiction to a forest and the reader to a wanderer. For Eco,

> a wood is a garden of forking paths. Even when there are no well-trodden paths in a wood, everyone can trace his or her own path, deciding to go to the left or to the right of a certain tree and making a choice at every tree encountered.[34]

Following a path is a convenient way to travel in a forest. But sometimes we see interesting things elsewhere and need to depart from the existing path or the direction we were heading. The uncertainty of our precise location and the relief it gives us may be part of a recreational pursuit and nature appreciation. In art appreciation, in turn, it seems that a departure from the path is not recommended, for there may be beasts lurking in the bushes: these are creatures of our own imagination.

Imagination and fantasy

Fiction has not always fared well in aesthetic and intellectual terms. A genre considered of low social and moral origin was not much appreciated in Europe in the beginning of the eighteenth century when it was associated with fantasizing and seen as a waste of time. *Lesesucht*, reading mania, was horrendous, and it was thought that reading would make people daydreamers. In 1740, Samuel Richardson made Pamela write a letter containing these words:

> [T]here were very few novels and romances that my lady would permit me to read; and those I did, gave me no great pleasure; for either they dealt so much in the *marvellous* and *improbable*, or were so unnaturally *inflaming* to the *passions*, and so full of *love* and *intrigue*, that most of them seemed calculated to *fire* the *imagination*, rather than to *inform* the *judgment*.[35]

Kirk Pillow remarks that '[a] centuries-old tradition associates imagining with madness [...], especially where imagination devolves into escapist and incommunicable fantasy or delusion'.[36] Suspicion of the literary imagination is old and largely parallels the rise of the reading public. Cervantes's *Don Quixote* ridiculed romantic stories in the seventeenth century; in the twentieth century, the realistic novel was considered an escapist and passive, bourgeois form of literature, entertainment that comforts the mind so as not to care about the anxieties of the world.

Yet, different forms of the imagination have been given different significance in the past. In his *Biographia Literaria* (1817), Samuel Taylor Coleridge made the famous distinction between *imagination* and *fancy*. For Coleridge, imagination is an important cognitive faculty which 'dissolves, diffuses, dissipates, in order to recreate'.[37] Fancy, in turn, plays with 'fixities and definites' and is no more than 'a mode of memory emancipated from the order of time and space' which 'must receive all its materials ready made from the law of association'.[38] Today, a similar distinction is made in aesthetics between *imagination* and *fantasy*. Kendall Walton, for example, holds that people may play all sorts of 'games' with a fictional work. In proper games of make-believe, however, the 'players are subject to prescriptions, deriving from rules of the games and the nature of the work, to imagine certain propositions – those that are fictional in the work'.[39] Some games, Walton maintains, are *unauthorized* by the work, or its misuse: they are against the *rules* or *conventions* about how the work is to be used.[40] These inappropriate games are akin to fantasies, in which dreamers indulge in their *dreams* and no longer pay attention to the props that make the *game*.[41]

Peter Lamarque and Stein Haugom Olsen, in turn, draw a distinction between fantasy and the mode of imagination associated with our response to artworks. They maintain that fantasy and art differ in that 'the former is self-centred, literally self-indulgent, while the latter seeks more detachment, a transcending of self-interest'.[42] Further, they think that at times one simply finds oneself in a certain state of mind (fantasy), whereas in imaginative responses to art one adopts a certain state of mind because one recognizes one is being invited to do so:

> In the case of works of art we respond in a certain way to fictive events (we *locate* ourselves in an imaginary world) at least partly because the recognition of the intention that we should respond in that way acts as a reason for our doing so. In contrast, the imaginings of fantasy are more manipulative; attitudes and responses are the product of *causes*; we adopt a point of view, as we might say, *in spite of ourselves*.[43]

Lamarque and Olsen maintain that in engaging with artworks, readers are or should be 'aware of how the structure of the work – its forms of expression, its use of literary convention – is controlling the perspective on offer'.[44] In fantasy, in turn, readers are only minimally aware of the representation embodying the fantasy. According to Lamarque and Olsen, imagination proper is 'to a large extent under the control of the author (and the work)', whereas fantasy is remote from literary appreciation.[45]

It is easy to agree with Walton and Lamarque and Olsen that in reading we are interested in what the work has to say – or even with constructivist views, enter into a dialogue with the work. Yet, it might not be reasonable to limit literary imagination to the imaginative response prompted by a work's fictional descriptions or draw a sharp line between prompted response and reflective supplementation of the content. It is traditionally thought that fantasizing moves one's attention away from the work, for example, to self-centric domains like dreams about one's life.[46] It is open to dispute, for instance, whether one's desire to be like a given character or one's wish for reality to be like the world of the work belongs to literary imagining or fantasizing. Sometimes a work may prompt the reader to look at the actual world through the literary representation.

Daydreaming might be more likely to occur in engagements with certain genres of fiction, namely, those that depict a setting and events remote from everyday life. Lamarque and Olsen propose that in genres, such as romance and fantasy, a condition for properly understanding the work – to appropriately supply the content with one's imagination – is that the reader projects herself into the world of the work using selective information about herself.[47] Such works of entertainment may be seen as prompted fantasy that is based on common dreams, like getting rich and famous or finding a perfect companion.

The imagination/fantasy distinction is a suitable tool for investigating our basic imaginary responses towards *fiction*. However, when we approach a work as a *literary* work of art, and our engagement with it in terms of aesthetic experience, the role of imagination seems different.

The aesthetics of imagination

Some philosophers have proposed that we may approach works of fiction in two ways: engaging imaginatively with the content of the work and examining the work as an artefact. Kendall Walton, for instance, thinks that readers characteristically take a 'dual standpoint' on the fictive content and consider themselves both inside and outside the fictional world.[48] Readers *participate* in the game of make-believe and *observe* the ways by which the fictional world is created (e.g. literary descriptions).[49] For Walton, this is 'one of the most fundamental and important features of the human institution of fiction'.[50]

Nevertheless, Walton says relatively little about the two standpoints, whereas Lamarque and Olsen exhaustively explore their related distinction between the *fictive stance* and the *literary stance*, which readers adopt in reading literary works of an imaginative kind.[51] Lamarque and Olsen consider the distinction between the fictive stance and the literary stance extremely important for our understanding of literary fictions. In their view, the fictive stance is, broadly speaking, about imagining the content of the work – the prompted imaginative response – whereas the literary stance is about recognizing and appreciating the aesthetic value of the work's development of its themes.[52] There are two sorts of responses thus involved: first, an imaginative response to fiction, that is, towards creations of imagination (from novels to scientific thought-experiments), and, second, a response towards works of art (fictional and non-fictional).

Lamarque and Olsen maintain that in reading works of literature, we imagine the content of the work (the fictive stance) put forward from a certain *point of view* and with a certain *tone* (the literary point of view). Elsewhere, Lamarque states that the response literary works call for is characteristically 'perspectival'. He speaks of the 'opacity' of literary narratives, claiming that 'tone, irony, humour, connotation, allusion, narrative voice and other aspects of representation colour all narrative that aspires to literary status'.[53] Yet, Lamarque and Olsen maintain that in reading works of literature, our imagination is under authorial control: in evaluating and appreciating the *work's perspective*.

Since Kant, aesthetic experience has been associated with the free play of cognitive faculties. In modernity, in turn, art is linked to challenges and unexpectedness; in reading a literary fiction, we are not just given a 'report' and our task is not only to make-believe its content, but we are presented with an object that requires interpretation and active participation: something new, unpredicted, uncommon. Artworks, unlike works of entertainment, also tend to resist pre-existing determinations, and in experimental cases even establish the very categories that are required for their understanding.[54] Analytic philosophers, in turn, have typically been interested in imagination as an *attitude* – a stance we take towards the content of a work of fiction, a form of attention, a way of holding something in the mind – rather than an *activity*, commonly coupling literary imagination with the imaginative supplementation of character and plot and exploring it as a story-level phenomenon (as Iser also did in his theory of gaps). When we look at critical interpretation of literary works, we see that they call for, and reward, more imaginative efforts.

Literary imagination is best understood as an activity that is guided by literary practice.[55] While imagination is present virtually everywhere, it is used for different purposes in different practices and has different directions or aims within these practices. We have different expectations about and interests in the content when approaching different sorts of works (fiction or non-fiction), and these expectations guide our attention in reading.[56] There is imagination that is constrained by truth and aims at truth, which we employ when we seek to understand how a given machine works or when we try to assemble furniture, for instance. There is also a mode of imagination that combines particular instances with abstract ideas, which we employ when we interpret an artwork or characterize a natural environment from an aesthetic point of view.

Stacie Friend and Derek Matravers argue that imagination is not to be associated with fiction but *narrative*. They remark that stories prompt imagining, regardless of their status as fiction or non-fiction, and argue that we do not need to know whether a narrative is non-fictional or fictional in order to engage with it or to comprehend or understand it.[57] Narratives are, however, many in kind, and literary-fictional narratives differ qualitatively from non-fictional narratives such as biographies, and especially from everyday or real-life narratives, the stories we tell about ourselves and others. Literary narratives contain thick descriptions of the thoughts and actions of the characters, and their narrative structures are complex. In addition to intrinsic differences between narratives, we seek different things in different sorts of narratives.

A work's status affects how we engage with it. For example, we assess a character's actions differently in literary and real-life narratives (think of Bartleby or Josef K., for instance). We evaluate the overall meaning of individual events differently in literary and real-life narratives. Assumedly, there is also a difference in our moral concerns in reading fiction and non-fiction; we can easily identify or sympathize with the bad guys in fiction, as we are temporarily disconnected from ourselves (or social norms) and perhaps taking an imaginative role ourselves, which is not, supposedly, likely to happen when we read non-fictional narratives on true crimes.

In literary imagining, aesthetic and genre conventions characteristically guide our expectations, whereas we assess, say, journalistic narratives with regard to their truthfulness (or informative success). Or let us consider Searle's 'Chinese Room' – a fiction within a philosophical journal article. Who is the speaker and why is he or she locked in the room? Who gives him or her the Chinese writing? What is the Chinese writing? Who are 'these people' and what is 'the program'? Is the speaker sane? These would be perfectly reasonable questions if the work was a literary work and not a philosophical thought-experiment. In turn, for a philosophical thought-experiment, the questions are irrelevant and utterly stupid.

The question of genre also affects our need for resolution. In art, we are interested in the development of the setting and tend to look for a closure or 'answer' of some sort.[58] Literary worlds are made in fictional descriptions, and the reader's interest is sustained by controlling and playing with her expectations. Standard newspaper reports, in turn, are structured according to conventional formats, such as the classic 'inverted pyramid' model in which the information is given in descending order, the most important points at the top of the article.

Yet, we allow more ambiguity in our engagement with literary narratives. Call it the poetic licence, suspension of disbelief, fictional pact, whatever; literary imagining is more charitable than the mode of imagination applied in reading non-literary narratives. In literary narratives, we allow various sorts of deviations and we tolerate inconsistent or unreliable reports of the events.[59] With certain narratives, we are not dissatisfied but delighted with mystery or perplexity with regard to the story – are the events happening for 'real' or are they part of the narrator's wishes or dreams or fears?

In literature, we have to accept the multiplicity of interpretations and ambiguous endings. In newspaper reports, in turn, we go on to look for more information elsewhere. Moreover, it is a different thing to read a murder story in which the murderer is a fictional character – and a report in which the murderer is real and on the loose. Whether there are differences in our emotional engagement with the narratives would be an interesting empirical question, but as for imaginative (narrative) engagement, there are dissimilarities: the former narrative is a closed system and does not prompt speculation about the future unlike the latter. The same goes for a narrative about a missing person. In a literary work, we are given 'all there is', whereas in a non-fictional narrative about a real person we are tempted to search for more information.

Many would consider our search for symbolic and thematic content as the *differentia specifica* of our engagement with literary works and artworks in general. It has been proposed that our search for themes of universal interest distinguishes our imaginative attitude to (fictional) literature from the attitude(s) we adopt towards non-*literary* texts; that our search for character development, narrative coherence and closure, universal themes and the like sets the literary stance apart from the attitude we adopt towards a newspaper report.[60]

Such a view finds support from criticism. For instance, in his review of Jonathan Littell's *Kindly Ones* (2009; *Les Bienveillantes*, 2006), the critic Jason Burke says that

> The novel is also a gripping military adventure story and a study in collective pathology. Above all, it is a sophisticated exploration of issues of morality, evil and luck. Littell told interviewers that the character of Aue allowed him to examine what he himself might have done had he been born in different circumstances at a different time. In the preface, Aue assumes a creepy complicity between himself and his readers. [. . .] Littell's point is that there is no firm line separating ordinary people from those responsible for acts such as the Holocaust. There is no absolute evil, banal or otherwise. There are, as Aue says, simply 'reasons, good or bad [. . .] human reasons'.[61]

Another critic, Tim Martin, writes that

> Much criticism has focused on the character of Aue, whose sexual interests and dedicated classicism threaten to draw the clichéd parallel between Nazism and perversity, refuting his claims to be 'just like us'. But *The Kindly Ones* never sets out to be the tale of a Nazi Everyman, a story of the banality of evil: it leaves that to the wealth of documentary testimony and factual commentary on the war. Instead, it is a magnificently artificial project in character construction, a highly literary and provocative attempt to create a character various enough to match the many discontinuous

realities of the apocalyptic Nazi world-view. The result is a sprawling, daring, loose-ended monster of a book, one that justifies its towering subject matter by its persistent and troubling refusal to offer easy answers and to make satisfying sense.[62]

These critics explore universal themes the work is about – global themes, such as 'morality, evil and luck', and a local theme, 'the many discontinuous realities of the apocalyptic Nazi world-view' – and present their somewhat conflicting views of the thematic claim the work implies or refuses to make: Burke on 'Littell's point' and Martin on the work's 'refusal to offer easy answers and to make satisfying sense'.

Of course, we may read works of history in order to understand the human need for mythical origins for a nation, or stories about fashion and lifestyle to learn what they reveal about our time – or, say, about vanity or pretension more general. Moreover, one could claim that our interest in non-literary (non-fictional) works goes beyond the particular, concrete matter explored in the work, or that we tend to look for abstract themes everywhere.

It is open to dispute whether our search for thematic meanings has to do with *artification* and *dramatization* or if it is due to authors' bringing *literary* features and *artistic* devices to non-fictional writing. Today, publishers encourage us to look for symbolic meaning or thematic content in, say, popular works of history. For example, Dan Jones's *The Plantagenets: The Warrior Kings and Queens Who Made England* (Penguin 2013) is advertised as an 'epic narrative history of courage, treachery, ambition, and deception' in which the author 'resurrects the unruly royal dynasty that preceded the Tudors'.[63] Some have used these sorts of marketing descriptions as evidence in arguing for the similarity between fictional and non-fictional imagination.[64] While such descriptions and other paratexts may encourage abstract imagining and reflection, they might rather characterize how non-fiction has become more entertainment-like than illuminate our engagement with non-fictional narratives in general. Perhaps the distinction is that our looking for abstract themes is an essential part of a literary response but only contingent (and reader-relative) in our engagement with non-literary narratives.

But what notions such as *appropriateness* and *appropriate response* have to do with art in the first place? We may, for instance, set aside questions about truth when we listen to entertaining anecdotes – even if their truth were very important for the teller. Further, our interest in a narrative work and our criteria of assessment may change while reading it. Individual works may also transgress conventional boundaries. Our initial conception of the genre of the text may prove inappropriate, and we may need to infer the appropriate (or most rewarding) way of reading from the text. The question is about aesthetic or intellectual or emotional reward. Sometimes a game gets better with new rules.

Interpretation and use

Umberto Eco, the proponent of the idea of the 'open work', thinks that literary works are open to infinite possibilities.[65] Eco, who is very fond of interpretative games both in his theories and fictions, recounts in his *Interpretation and Overinterpretation* (1992) how he initially found Jorge Luis Borges's 'Pierre Menard's' proposal to read Thomas à Kempis's *The Imitation of Christ* (*Imitatio Christi*, c. 1418–27) as if the work was written by Louis-Ferdinand Céline (1894–1961) an amusing idea and worth trying. Nevertheless, he came to conclude that the Menardian strategy works only with a small part of the content. For the most part of the work, such a reading was not fruitful and the work 'resisted the reading'.[66]

Related to the distinction between imagination and fantasy drawn in theories of fiction, a distinction between the *interpretation* and *use* of a work is often made in theories of literary interpretation. Eco also distinguishes between interpretation and use and, relying on Richard Rorty, he maintains that to critically interpret a text is 'to discover, along with our reactions to it, something about its nature', whereas to use a text is to 'start from it in order to get something else, even accepting the risk of misinterpreting it from the semantic point of view'.[67] For Eco, interpretation has to recognize the context of the work. While one may use a poem by Wordsworth for parody or to get inspiration for one's own musing, its interpretation requires that one must respect Wordsworth's 'cultural and linguistic background'.[68] In interpreting Wordsworth's poem we may not, for instance, give the words in the text meanings that they did not have in the poet's time.

Nonetheless, Eco thinks that interpretation and use are 'abstract theoretical possibilities' and that every empirical reading is an 'unpredictable mixture' of both: one's use of a text may eventually end in a fruitful new interpretation, or an interpretation may turn into use. Moreover, Eco argues that sometimes we need to use texts in order to

> free them from previous interpretations, to discover new aspects of them, to realize that before they had been illicitly interpreted, to find out a new and more explicative *intentio operis*, that too many uncontrolled intentions of the readers (perhaps disguised as a faithful quest for the intention of the author) had polluted and obscured.[69]

It is also questionable if we can differentiate between our various motives to read – and if we are interpreting or using a work in reading it. We grab books for various reasons: in addition to aesthetic enjoyment, we want to enlarge our cultural competence, to do something that helps us to concentrate; or we want to be a part of a given community by knowing what 'unbearable lightness' is. In the practice of reading, intrinsic and instrumental purposes go together and interpretation and use mix.

Fiction and reflection

Another issue with 'bound imagination' concerns the reader's 'external considerations': her reflecting the content of the work in relation to reality. As said, the paradigmatic analytic theories of fiction define the audience's appropriate attitude towards a fictional work in terms of make-believe. When reading fictional literature, the theories propose, readers are basically to make-believe the propositional content of the work and its truth and reference. Nevertheless, imaginative engagement with a work of literary fiction commonly involves, and sometimes arguably necessitates, readers reflecting on the fictional content in different ways in relation to reality. Analytic philosophers maintain that there are two different ways to approach and speak of the content of a work of fiction such as true propositions and apparent authorial assertions in the work. Walton and Currie make a distinction between *imagination (make-believe)* and *belief/disbelief*, whereas Lamarque and Olsen speak of the audience's *internal* and *external perspectives* on the fictional content (in addition to the audience's fictive stance and literary stance).

Imaginative engagement with a work of fiction characteristically involves readers reflecting on the content of the work, that is, sentences, passages or utterances in the story, in relation to reality, or drawing on their beliefs about the actual world.[70] As suggested earlier, different literary genres supposedly emphasize different kinds of imagining, and different modes of reading set different interests and significance for so-called worldly considerations, that is, for reflecting how the content of the work figures outside the fictional realm.

The elementary need for drawing from actual world beliefs in imaginative engagement with fiction relates to implied fictional truths and their imaginative supplementation, as Ingarden and Iser have demonstrated. Readers fill in the gaps in the narrative partly with their knowledge about reality. This activity is, however, to a large degree spontaneous and unnoticeable and does not require the involvement of worldly considerations in the sense of reflecting on the fictional setting in the light of the actual world or, say, comparing the two. The reader simply applies her actual beliefs, such as her basic beliefs concerning human behaviour, to the story.

On a more conscious level, a reader may feel the need to speculate or reason about a character's motives and actions – for example, in the light of her folk psychological knowledge – in order to comprehend the character and the story events. Acknowledging the need for this kind of external consideration, which often comes in the form of a problem, is not unusual in theories of literary interpretation. In his philosophical theory of fiction, Walton goes so far as to maintain that if one is ascertaining a work's implicit fictional truths, such as the reason for a character's antisocial behaviour, even by making a library visit and consulting medical studies on neurological diseases (extrapolation based on what he calls the 'Reality Principle') or historical sources concerning mutual religious beliefs in the author's society (extrapolation based on what he calls the 'Mutual Belief Principle'), one is still participating in a game of make-believe.[71]

There are also different kinds of communication that authors may aim to perform in or through their works. By their fictional representations, authors may, for instance, make or imply assertions or perhaps advance hypotheses, provide insights or encourage understanding, or intend to draw the audience's attention to states of affairs in the actual world. This sort of authorial communication is perhaps best seen on an arbitrary scale ranging from explicit assertions that are intended to be believed, and are characteristic for didactic fictions, to invitations to, for example, philosophical, moral, social or political contemplation which may serve informative or aesthetic purposes, that is, which may be intended to prompt extra-fictional considerations or strengthen readers' response to the fictional setting by means of their beliefs about reality.

Respectively, readers may have different kinds of cognitive intentions or expectations. They may purposely 'read for life',[72] with a motive for gaining understanding of reality or themselves. On the other hand, an aesthetic response may include reflection and self-reflection, as the reader's (or spectator's or hearer's) monitoring of her own responses, perhaps leading her to a refined understanding of different emotions, for instance.[73] Readers who read Dostoyevsky or Tolstoy partly in order to gain insights about human life arguably read the works properly as works of literary fiction, assuming that they take them to be literally non-assertive.[74] Whether such cognitive expectations have a place in *literary* interpretation is, however, a matter of dispute. While a reader's cognitive expectations might be part of a literary response to the work, one has to admit that from a literary point of view, a reader whose only or main interest in a work of literature is in obtaining, say, psychological insights from the story, is not 'properly' attending to the work. The most controversial issue in the debate on the role of external considerations in reading is their role in *literary appreciation*, as in evaluating the significance of a literary theme or the way it is being developed in the work. As the act of imaginatively engaging with a work (of fiction) is generally distinguished from the act of evaluating the work as a literary work, I shall discuss these questions, *imaginative engagement* and *appreciation*, separately.

In the make-believe theories, readers' external considerations of fictional matters are commonly discussed in terms of readers' belief or disbelief in fictional propositions. While the theories maintain that to engage with a fictional story is to imagine, make-believe or pretend that its propositional content is true and to set aside questions of truth and reality, Walton and Currie, for instance, argue not only that a reader may simultaneously make-believe and believe a fictional proposition but also that an author may intend an utterance in her work, or perhaps her whole work, to be both made-believe and believed.[75] As noted, Walton and Currie say relatively little of the role of external considerations in literary interpretation, whereas Lamarque and Olsen discuss the topic extensively.[76]

Lamarque and Olsen maintain that readers may take a dual perspective on the fictional content of a work. In their view, certain kinds of descriptions in fiction invite both internal and external reflection.[77] As one of their examples, they use the narrator's generalization about 'shallow natures' in George Eliot's *Middlemarch*. Lamarque and Olsen assert that when reflected on from the internal perspective, the generalization enhances the reader's understanding of a fictional character, Rosamund Vincy, whom the generalization concerns, while reflecting on the generalization from the external perspective 'involves thinking of "shallow natures"' beyond the fictional setting.[78] Although Lamarque and Olsen say that these perspectives 'nicely interact', they take the external perspective to have a narrow and limited role in the literary-fictive response.[79] They give the external perspective this limited role because they find that generalizations and other explicit or implicit propositions in fiction are 'almost never to be taken at face value, merely as general assertions about the world issued directly by the author'.[80] As they see it, such a response would be 'to abandon the cognitive distance of the fictive stance'.[81] As for literary interpretation, the interest which generalizations have from the external perspective is, for them, 'conditioned by their role under the internal perspective'.[82] In Lamarque and Olsen's view, to reflect on a general proposition in a work of fiction from the external perspective is to consider it for its truth, or truth-*conditions*, which serves to enhance fictional characterization.[83]

The distinction between the internal and the external perspective is extremely helpful in clarifying the discourse about fictional works and objects. However, the external perspective is arguably much more complicated and has a greater role in the general reading public's literary experience than Lamarque and Olsen propose. The internal and the external perspectives on the fictional content of a work likely admit both different degrees and different modes, depending on the type of the work. When it comes to the internal perspective employed in an engagement with a literary fiction, *de se* imagining, visual imagining and affective response are certainly characteristic of, but none of them perhaps necessary for, the perspective. An imaginative engagement with a highly dramatic and emotional narrative differs from that with a work that contains large amounts of, say, explicit philosophical speculation, both for the *interaction* between the internal and external perspectives and for the *kinds* and *intensity* of imagining. Metafictional novels, in turn, often exploit and ridicule the (fictional) reader's expectations that are a product of her encounters with vivid and coherent realistic works, whereas Epic Theatre aimed to get rid of even escapist make-believe and keep the spectator constantly aware of the fictionality of the play she was watching.[84]

Conversely, external considerations seem to come with different propositional attitudes and might involve different mental processes from supposing a proposition via determining its truth-conditions to ultimately assessing its truth-value. Furthermore, the reader's act of externally reflecting on the fictional content, even considering it for its truth, may be seen to admit to degrees with regard to her engagement with the story or 'transportation' to it (the internal perspective). There are authors' explicit assertions in fictions, especially in those of the didactic sort, which the author clearly intends the reader to believe and which could be assessed outright without endangering the 'cognitive distance' of the fictive stance too much. For instance, the assertion which Voltaire conveys by presenting Pangloss's speeches and his misfortune in *Candide*, namely, that Leibniz's metaphysics is ridiculous, may be recognized as a genuine assertion while engaging with the fictional story. In more 'literary' cases, in turn, there seems to be less legitimate space for external considerations, at least for those in which the fictional content would be formulated as assertions by the author or the work and assessed for their truth. This means that as readers pay attention to the ways by which, say, philosophical views are being thematically developed in the work, their focus of imagining is in the internal perspective, and their external considerations primarily feed the comprehension of the story, as Lamarque and Olsen propose.

Perhaps their place is elsewhere. Peter Kivy has suggested that while a reader's external considerations might not have a place in the very act of following the story, that is, an imaginative engagement with it, the considerations may still be considered part of the encounter with the work. Kivy remarks that there is a distinctive temporal dimension in literary experience, as large novels, for instance, are typically read in parts. According to him, external considerations take place in the 'gaps' and 'afterlife' of the literary experience, that is, between the readings of a work and after it has been finished. Kivy argues that 'it is in the gaps in literary time [. . .] that the reader is meant to think about this material, *as part of the literary experience*'.[85] He maintains that gaps in literary experience provide an 'opportunity for thought about the matter that one has read; both the nature of the narrative events themselves, and whatever philosophical, moral, psychological or other such theses the author intends to convey in her work'.[86] Kivy maintains that when the reader is contemplating an issue – a hypothesis – raised by the work after reading it, she is still enjoying the work, external considerations thus being part of literary appreciation.

Kivy makes an important point. Works as extensive as novels are not devoured at once, and they live with us during the gaps in the literary experience and after we have finished them. There is place for the imagination in supplementing the narrative content while reading – and reflecting on it while not reading. An insightful literary representation of, say, people living a hectic urban life may make one ponder the author's point with regard to what one sees in one's daily life, perhaps to look around in the subway train in which one is reading the book or thinking about it. When one is impressed by a work, one may temporarily adopt the author's perspective towards the world and see how it fits in. (Reservations about this view will be discussed in Chapter 3.)

The aftertaste of a literary experience might linger for a long time and a work may have a serious impact on the reader. Many can name formative works that have shaped their attitudes in their youth. Some works even become companions that travel with the readers for their whole life. However, a work – a memory of it – may start to live its own life. It is a common phenomenon that an insight or saying we look for in a book we have read is not quite like we thought it was (or perhaps even there). When we read a novel the second time, we may become baffled, as we notice that it does not correspond with our memory of it. Similarly, it is a commonplace that recalling and retelling a story affects the original memory. Literary stories, even what we read yesterday, soon get a new structure (or at least a new emphasis about what was relevant in it) in our minds. Like imagination and fantasy and interpretation and use, memory and invention cannot be completely separated either – a topic explored in Chapter 3.

3

Narrative

It has become a commonplace that narrative plays an important, even essential role in our understanding of reality and ourselves. We constantly hear that we experience the world as narratives and communicate our experiences by them; that our memories of the past, our explanations of the present, and our plans for the future take the form of a story.[1] The great story of our time is story itself.[2] Narrative is repeatedly claimed to be our most fundamental form of processing, organizing and communicating information. For instance, the cognitive scientist Mark Turner states that 'most of our experience, our knowledge, and our thinking is organized as stories'.[3] For him, 'narrative imagining – story – is the fundamental instrument of thought. Rational capacities depend upon it. It is our chief means of looking into the future, of predicting, of planning, and of explaining. It is a literary capacity indispensable to human cognition generally.'[4]

Turner indeed thinks that everyday narrative imagining is a *literary* capacity. And he is not alone: the philosopher Alasdair MacIntyre, for one, believes that people understand themselves and their lives as narratives; for MacIntyre, even ordinary conversations are *dramatic* works, which have their beginnings, middles and ends.[5] In turn, the philosopher Daniel Dennett makes an analogy between selfhood and artistry, claiming that 'we are all virtuoso novelists', as 'we try to make all of our material cohere into a single good story', namely, our autobiography, in which the 'chief fictional character is one's self'.[6] Jonathan Glover, a philosopher too, thinks that 'self-creation tends to make a life like a novel by a single author'.[7] The psychologist Jerome Bruner goes even further in claiming that narrative does not only represent reality but also constitutes it. In his view, we organize our experience in narrative form and, further, 'our experience of human affairs comes to take the form of the narratives we use in telling about them'.[8] For Bruner, stories 'impose a structure, a compelling reality on what we experience'.[9]

But there is suspicion, too, about narrative. Literary narratologists have been dissatisfied in the wide, superficial use of the concept of narrative in social sciences and the inflation thus caused: they have spoken of 'narrative hegemony' (Martin Kreiswirth) and 'narrative imperialism' (James Phelan), which both lose what is distinctive of narrative and flatten the phenomenon studied.[10] A related concern in literary studies is that narrative imperialism reduces all the diversity and polyphony of literature into ideal models, schemas, and stereotypes. In analytic philosophy, in turn, there has been scepticism about the very concept of narrative and its explanatory power: philosophers have argued that narrative is difficult to define and that appeal to it does not add much to our explanations of human action.[11]

This chapter explores the epistemic significance of narratives. I will first examine the recent philosophical criticism against self-narratives and views on the potential dangers of artistic narratives, arguing that the critique builds on problematic assumptions about narrative. Second, I will propose that the narrow concept of *knowledge* applied in the debate is unsuccessful in explaining our epistemically beneficial use of narratives in our lives and that we should approach narrative cognition in terms of *understanding*. Finally, I will illustrate how the debate on the epistemic value of stories, everyday and literary, takes a new course with the concept of understanding.

Narrative knowledge and living stories

The critics of narrative explanations and narrative conceptions of personhood in particular object to the idea that one's self could be made into a story. Self-narratives, the stories we tell about ourselves, are said to be situational. It is claimed, for instance, that one's condition affects how one understands and tells one's life. The critics are not concerned with the reality of the events themselves – a divorce, the death of a child, move to another city – but the selection of the events included in the story, the teller's understanding of them (such as the motives the teller sees guiding her and others' actions), the significance given for them and the attitude taken towards them. The content of self-narratives and the teller's interpretation and evaluation of the events are said to vary with regard to the purpose of the story, the context of the telling, the audience (real persons or imaginary readers) and the like. Even more: who is really familiar with herself, the critics ask. In addition to psychoanalysis, a recent study in neurosciences is used to support critics' doubt on people's self-understanding.

We have various stories of ourselves. The philosopher Peter Lamarque remarks that we 'return to the major events in our lives and recount them over and over in different narratives from different points of view', which in his view makes the idea of unity and coherence crumble away.[12] Lamarque claims that 'the more important the event, the more perspectives it invites, thus the more narratives we relate, often in conflict with each other'.[13] For him, narrative does not produce unity or personal identity but presupposes it; people who tell stories of themselves already have a strong sense of self, whereas 'those of us without any such self-assurance will hesitate to embark on a grand self-narrative, being too aware of the tensions, inconsistencies and multiple personalities in our lives'.[14] If we want to use an artistic analogy, we ought to follow Roland Barthes and say that we are not the protagonist of a novel but the whole cast in it.[15]

Our understanding of the significance of past events in our lives and their impact on us changes as our (self-)knowledge develops. We are able to explain some of our actions only afterwards. When being active participants, living our lives forward, we might not have been able to properly reflect our doings. On the other hand, our memories change, and our stories of the past may be anachronistic. The philosopher Peter Goldie asserts that 'the demands of narrativity [...] seem to drag us towards thinking of our past thoughts, feelings, and deliberations as more determinate than they in fact were, and as reflective of an agency of which at the time we seemed quite bereft'.[16] Epiphany, the moment of critical discovery or revelation – 'the moment I realised that' – hardly exists in life as clearly as in dramatic stories we tell afterwards.

For *the* story-critical philosopher Galen Strawson, a major worry with self-narratives is our tendency to *revision*: to 'engage unconsciously in invention, fiction of some sort – falsification, confabulation, revisionism – when it comes to one's apprehension of one's own life'.[17] Strawson argues that one's 'telling and retelling one's past leads to changes, smoothings, enhancements, shifts away from the facts'.[18] This means, he claims, that 'the more you recall, retell, narrate yourself, the further you risk moving away from accurate self-understanding, from the truth of your being'.[19] The talk of the 'truth of one's being' brings along extensive questions – Is personality something innate and stable? How experiences exist before they are told or thought? – but Strawson's remark of revision in storytelling describes a phenomenon familiar to many. Primo Levi, the Italian author known especially for his holocaust memories, says in an oft-cited passage of *The Drowned and Saved* that

> The memories which lie within us are not carved in stone; not only do they tend to become erased as the years go by, but often they change, or even grow, by incorporating extraneous features. [...] Certainly practice (in this case, frequent re-evocation) keeps

memories fresh and alive in the same manner in which a muscle often used remains efficient, but it is also true that a memory evoked too often, and expressed in the form of a story, tends to become fixed in a stereotype, in a form tested by experience, crystallized, perfected, adorned, installing itself in the place of the raw memory and growing at its expense.[20]

And whose memories actually are our memories? The sociologist Edward Shils notes that one's memory does not consist only of the recollections of personal experiences but from the memories of others, such as one's family members and friends.[21] One ought to add: as they remember and interpret those events. Narrative enthusiasts like to remind us that we are born in the middle of stories and that 'our story' begins before us (such as with the foreword written by our parents and the editor's note written by our older siblings). Our stories continue, respond to and challenge the stories other people tell about us.

Of course, a narrative needs to be narrated, and in public telling social norms and conventions guide storytelling: what one can tell and how – think of personal religious or sexual matters, for instance. In public self-narration, one's self seeks form and content from surrounding cultural models, such as a 'new mother', a 'failed businessman' and the like.[22] Self-narration follows historical and communal structures of meaning-giving.[23]

Moreover, storytelling has various functions. We tell stories to explain our choices and to illustrate our values to ourselves and others. We tell ironic, exaggerated stories of our failures to amuse our friends and sentimental, equally exaggerated stories of the same events to elicit their sympathy, both sort of stories (their public tellings) perhaps helping us to understand and overcome the events. Conformists among us stylize their stories to match the values of the context in order to produce social cohesion, spontaneously 'adjusting' their stories according to the audience's reactions.[24] Some others colour their stories to gain appreciation. Also, it is tempting to use narratives to affect people's attitudes;[25] after all, stories persuade better than rational arguments. We even use them on ourselves: we might underrate our shameful doings in a story as if the story could change the past. If you are aiming for self-deception, go with narrative.

It is often suggested that we constantly balance between accuracy and coherence in real-life storytelling: we want to be entertaining, but we would also like to be truthful. Akin to literary narratives, real-life narratives are built with expectations and twists: what we aimed for, what we expected, what could have happened and what ultimately happened.[26] This is required in order to maintain the audience's interest and to convey our expectations and intentions – not to mention emotions – at the time of experience. And in building this tension, the dramatic structures of artistic stories easily sneak in.

On the other hand, the context of telling sets the criteria for evaluation. Police interrogators believe that stories may be true or false, and so believe a poststructuralist when making a report of an offence. In turn, we are charitable to a person who in her autobiography embellishes her life and 'forgets' certain incidents in her past, for it is so human.[27] In our everyday life, we hear all sorts of anecdotes and gossips, which we value as informative or entertaining, depending on the context and our interests. Narratives draw us in many directions. But the critics of narrative think that things may get really bad if we bring artistic and real-life stories too close together.

Doubts about literary narratives

Lamarque has extensively criticized views that seek to understand real lives in terms of literary narratives. He contends that literary narratives and our real-life narratives are qualitatively different. For him, the content of a literary work is 'perspectival' and essentially given from a particular point of view. This 'opacity', as he calls it, 'runs deep in narrative representation: tone, irony, humour, connotation, allusion, narrative voice and other aspects of representation colour all narrative that aspires to literary status. Or, more accurately, one should say that readers come to literary works with an expectation, that narrative perspective of this kind is salient, that the modes of representation are significant.'[28]

Because of the opacity of literary narratives, Lamarque is sceptical of the view that works of literature could directly aid our conception of self, for instance, by offering paradigmatic character types and guiding our behaviour, or by shaping our lives through their structures and plots.[29] He thinks that if literary works are taken as models for real-life narratives, they are read in superficial ways or 'transparently', 'as works to look through but not at'.[30] However, Lamarque argues that when we attend to the works as works of literature – that is, opaquely – the parallels with our lives appear strained.[31] He claims that to see fictional characters as ordinary people, and their lives essentially like ours, is to 'ignore all essentially literary qualities and reduce literature to character and plot at the same level of banality as found in the stories we tell of ourselves'.[32]

In this view, Nelson Goodman would be trivializing matters when saying that '"Don Quixote", taken literally, applies to no one, but taken figuratively, applies to many of us – for example, to me in my tilts with the windmills of current linguistics'.[33] Superficial would also be Arthur C. Danto, who says that

> [T]he greatest metaphors of art I believe to be those in which the spectator identifies himself with the attributes of the represented character: and sees his or her life in terms of the life depicted: it is oneself as Anna Karenina, or Isabelle Archer, or Elizabeth Bennet, or O: oneself sipping limetea; in the Marabar Caves; in the waters of East Egg; in the Red Chamber . . . where the artwork becomes a metaphor for life and life is transfigured. [. . .] [A]rtistic metaphors

[. . .] are in some way true: to see oneself as Anna is in some way to *be* Anna, and to see one's life as *her* life, so as to be changed by experience of being her.[34]

Lamarque claims that when we consider iconic literary characters as abstractions and apply them to the real world, we come 'to lose everything that makes them literary in the first place', namely, their characteristics crafted in nuanced fictional descriptions.[35] Moreover, he emphasizes that everything in literary narratives serves aesthetic (or dramatic) purposes: from an external point of view, the reasons which fictional characters have for their actions are chosen to meet 'aesthetic, structural and genre-based demands for works of that kind', which means that in literary narratives every detail is *created* and has relevance with regard to the overall design of the work.[36]

These distinctive features of literary narratives lead Lamarque to conclude that modelling our lives on literary narratives would distort our understanding of reality and ourselves.[37] More precisely, it would lead us to (i) seek meaning where there is mere coincidence, to (ii) let formal structures dictate action instead of rational choice, to (iii) aestheticize our lives and to (iv) impose a 'false teleology' on our lives.[38] Explanations based on literary narratives might lead to self-deception, such as confabulation; one's considering oneself as a character in a plot would, in turn, be 'self-aggrandisement'.[39] Moreover, a 'literary' view of life could constrain one's action and undermine one's sense of being in control of one's life, as one starts to drift the way demanded by the 'genre' (e.g. tragedy) and the 'plot' (perhaps including elements such as *hubris*, *hamartia*, *peripeteia*, *nemesis*, *anagnorisis* and *catharsis*) – as in Freudian 'fate neurosis' (*Schicksalneurose*). And while literary narratives have a dramatic closure, Lamarque argues that real lives 'just "terminate", quite often *in medias res*'.[40]

A truth is that real-life narratives and literary narratives are radically different. But it is equally true that we, or many of us, have a tendency to give our experiences, memories and plans a story form. We use narrative in giving meaning (conceivability) and significance (value). Reality is a chaotic and incomprehensible flow if we have no conception of causality, and life is dull and meaningless without purposeful action. In his classic work *The Sense of an Ending* (1967) Frank Kermode says that we cannot stand the 'nauseous and viscous' contingency of reality.[41] We cannot bear the randomness or uncertainty of life but need sense, structure and aim. We strive for a closure – which may be emotional, a mere *feeling* of this being it.[42] This is important especially in traumatic cases. What happened to a missing person? We accept a judgement made of a speculation: so it must have been. The need for stories is existential: literature fulfils – and disturbs – this longing for sense.

From knowledge to understanding

The critics of narrative explanations and narrative conceptions of personhood base their criticism on a conception of narrative that is defined in terms of plot and emphasizes unity and coherence. In Lamarque's view,

> The impression given by the term 'narrative' is of a complete, rounded story with a beginning, middle and end that helps make sense of complex events. The model is historical narrative or the complex narratives of fiction. But personal narratives virtually never attain completeness, closure or unity.[43]

Nevertheless, in recent decades plot-based conceptions have been contested in narrative theorizing in literary studies as well as social sciences,[44] and they have been challenged with models that conceive narrative, or rather, narrativity (which comes in degrees) primarily in terms of a representation of anthropomorphic experientiality.[45] The idea that the paradigmatic historical or literary narrative – or the ideal model for a personal narrative – is 'a complete, rounded story with a beginning, middle and end' has long been questioned. Mark Freeman, for one, criticizes a narrow, univocal way of speaking about narrative – and also warns us about proclamations about what *life* is like:

> For some, the term [narrative] connotes the existence of tidy tales, with discrete beginnings, middles, and ends; if that is the case, one is bound to see a significant disjunction between life and narrative. The reason is clear: generally speaking, our lives are *not* tidy tales; they are frequently rather messy and may be emplotted in lots of different ways. If, on the other hand, one is operating with a more post-modern or post-structuralist conception of narrative and is attentive to margins, breaks, fissures, and so on, then one might actually see more congruence between life and narrative: messy, discontinuous, incoherent stories for messy, discontinuous, incoherent lives.[46]

Another debatable idea – one that I will explore in what follows – is the view that the epistemic value of narrative lies in its ability to record events. When we approach narrative as a vehicle for understanding, the matter looks different.

Indeed, in narrative theory deriving from the hermeneutic and phenomenological tradition, self-narration is seen not as reconstruction but construction. Paul Ricœur, for one, says that 'we recognize ourselves in the stories that we tell about ourselves. It makes very little difference whether these stories are true or false, fiction as well as verifiable history provides us with an identity.'[47] We change constantly, and (self-)narration is continuous (re-)interpretation. The literary critic Paul John Eakin argues that 'autobiographical truth is not a fixed but an evolving content in an intricate process of self-discovery and self-creation.'[48] The philosopher Anthony Kerby, in turn, proposes that we should speak of the 'pragmatic and relative adequacy' of real-life narratives, for 'narrative truths' are 'more a matter of facilitating understanding and integration than of generating strict historical verisimilitude'.[49] This is not to say that autobiography is indifferent to truth,[50] but that from the viewpoint of cognition, narratives are not (mere) records of events.

In epistemology and philosophy of science, philosophers such as Catherine Elgin, Neil Cooper, Jonathan Kvanvig and Linda Zagzebski have emphasized the value of *understanding* in our cognitive endeavours and thus come near to the hermeneutic and phenomenological tradition. As they see it, understanding is more important than possessing individual truths and knowledge. Systematizing roughly their views, they hold that

(i) Understanding is holistic; it concerns the whole phenomenon and cannot be broken into bits.[51]
(ii) Understanding is seeing and creating connections between bits of knowledge.[52] It is about grasping explanatory and other coherence-making relationships in a large body of information; and about seeing.[53]
(iii) Understanding is giving significance to individual truths.[54] Cognitive progress is not only about gaining new information but deepening what we already know: evaluating the information we have at our disposal.
(iv) Understanding is (in some philosophers' view) non-factive.[55] Some truths may be trivial, whereas some falsehoods are useful approximations or idealizations (ideal gas or H_2O, for instance).[56] The advancement of understanding may require deliberate distortion, and accurate knowledge and understanding of the whole can draw us in opposite directions.[57]
(v) Understanding comes in degrees and is characteristically a process.[58]
(vi) Understanding is largely non-propositional. We understand automobile engines, diseases and the like.[59] The development

of understanding manifests itself in the ability to present new, insightful questions, for instance.[60]

(vii) Understanding can be achieved in many ways.[61] Alternative theories may improve our understanding of the same subject.[62] Maps can be drawn in various equally apt ways.

Narrative explanations and understanding seem close companions, as causality and evaluation play a central role in both of them. Narratives convey understanding, as they do not only store information but structure and value it; as Kerby remarks, 'in the telling we seem also to be immediately involved in generating the *value* of a certain state of affairs or course of action, of judging its worth, ethical or otherwise.'[63] The psychologist Donald Polkinghorne, in turn, suggests that

> storied memories retain the complexity of the situation in which an action was undertaken and the emotional and motivational meaning connected with it. Narrative cognition configures the diverse elements of a particular action into a unified whole in which each element is connected to the central purpose of the action.[64]

Nevertheless, the notion of understanding systematized earlier concerns primarily the natural world and paradigmatically scientific explanations. What is it to understand oneself or the social world?

Self is a complex aggregation of beliefs, emotions and attitudes. It would be challenging to speak of such an entity as *a whole*, as the notion of objectual understanding implies. What would the requirement of coherence that relates to (ideal) understanding then mean? Would holistic self-understanding be then something like a polyphonic novel – assuming that we humans, or at least many of us, are complex and inconsistent? Or is the object of self-understanding one's present self – one's uppermost attitudes, beliefs and emotions – or some aspect of the self, a personality trait, a way of behaving and the 'unity of life' only indirectly? Perhaps we should not ask too much from self-narratives or any other sort of explanations of the self.

Indeed, some have proposed that even brief narrative explanations could have an important role in enhancing our understanding of ourselves. Daniel Hutto, for one, argues for the value of 'small narratives' in self-narration, whereas David Cooper claims that we render our actions intelligible by 'little narratives'.[65] For example, narrative explanations, by which we illuminate our actions with respect to our values and purposes, are our attempts to understand ourselves and to communicate this understanding to others. Such narratives are often fragmentary, and their unity and coherence are ultimately brought in by the reader or hearer;[66] many of our stories are joint accomplishments and produced in dialogues. Also, we should be modest about the idea of *seeing connections*. None of us is able to name the 'relevant factors' that have contributed to making of our self, but many of us can tell illuminating stories of formative events, ideals, hopes and fears, influential persons, and the like, in our lives.

The idea of the potential value of *falsehoods* and *idealizations*, in turn, fits well with the common idea of self-narratives. Our earlier misconceptions of ourselves – those that we now acknowledge to be false – are an important part of our self-understanding and history.[67] Moreover, we make deliberate distortions in order to achieve cognitive ends, the falsehoods and idealizations serving our understanding of how things are.[68] For instance, I may think what I was like as a child and imagine being that child as a basis to understand my temper and ways of reacting today, yet acknowledging that my imaginative projection is a simplification. Of course, one's false beliefs about oneself, such as extreme confidence in one's abilities, may be pragmatically useful; still, they do not enhance but distort one's self-understanding. Idealizations are valuable when they are used as assumptions or hypotheses in an enterprise that aims at solving out how things are.

The *processual view* of understanding also suits the idea of narrative as a continuous social project. Jens Brockmeier and Hanna Meretoja aptly remark that understanding is not 'realized in a single act of comprehension. Subject to dialogue, conflict, and contest, it is a process carried out through revisions and reinterpretations that are, in principle, endless.'[69] Our views and attitudes change and develop. Understanding affects the understood, and we wander in a lifelong circle. Circle, indeed. How can I know for sure that my current self-understanding is more appropriate than the earlier? That I think of my earlier self-conceptions or ideas about myself as misguided in one way or another does not imply that they are such or that my new self-conceptions would be any more appropriate.

Nonetheless, it is important to note that while stories may carry misconceptions, that does not mean that the story form would be the (only) factor that distorts, say, 'the truth of our being'. Rather, *memory* and *reflection* already strongly bias self-misunderstanding. In exploring the value of self-examination in diminishing self-misunderstanding, the philosopher Hilary Kornblith argues that reflection is not the solution to the problem but rather an important source of it.[70] By telling stories, we bring our self-conceptions and self-misunderstanding, our complexities and inconsistencies, for others to comment, challenge, correct and complement.[71] The stories we tell reflect back to us as remarks and questions, facial gestures (and attempts to hide them), and meaningful silence.

Literary stories and self-understanding: Tentative remarks

As we think of cognition in terms of understanding, the question of the value of narrative now looks different. But where does that put literary narratives – the paradigmatic narratives? There are various ways to explore the value of literary narratives for their potential to contribute to our understanding of ourselves and reality. I propose that two aspects that ought to be paid attention in exploring the cognitive significance of literary narratives are *processuality* and *artificiality*. The former relates to our engaging with literary narratives and the latter to our exploring them as fabrications.

As noted, a chief fascination with narrative is its ability to embody emotional and motivational meanings and connect these to the actor's purpose.[72] Narrative illuminates structural dimensions, development and change. Peter Goldie emphasizes that an emotion such as *grief* should not be conceived as a mental state or event but a process, 'a complex pattern of activity and passivity, inner and outer, that unfolds over time'.[73] For Goldie, grief 'includes characteristic thoughts, judgements, feelings, memories, imaginings, actions, expressive actions, habitual actions, and much else besides, unfolding over time'.[74] Given their dramatic structures and the kind of engagement they invite, literary works provide us an insight into the processual dimension of emotions, such as the stages of grief and sorrow and the unfolding of actions like punishment or forgiving. As Zamir puts it, it is a commonplace that 'literature fosters a mode of attention and internalisation seldom reached elsewhere'.[75]

It even seems that certain actions and phenomena invite narrative explanation because of their nature; Ricœur famously states that 'the whole history of suffering cries out for vengeance and calls for narrative'.[76] Artistic narratives help us to understand such complex processes. Works such as *The Iliad, Hamlet, The Count of Monte Cristo* and 'The Cask of Amontillado' illuminate the abstract concept of vengeance – its motivational and emotional dimensions – and prompt moral philosophical thought on it.[77] Counter-narratives, in turn, resist dominant cultural narratives and make a place for those who do not grieve in the way expected, for example.

Yet, we should recall the remarks on the qualitative differences between real-life and literary narratives and notice the textuality of insights in literature; to pay attention to how the manner of representation shapes the content of a literary work.⁷⁸ Our worldly reflections ought to be sensitive to the textual and dramatic aspects of literary insights – the ideas we arrive at in reading literature. Rather than saying that literary narratives show or tell us *what* vengeance ultimately is, we might speak of an 'eye-opening effect' and evaluate our insights on functionalist criteria, by their ability to help us in formulating questions on the philosophy and psychology of vengeance, for example.

Moreover, when we explore literary narratives from an 'external' viewpoint, acknowledging their artificiality, we gain insight into literary schemes and techniques of storytelling that affect our everyday stories. Goldie suggests that by conceiving the differences between real-life narratives and literary narratives, we come to acknowledge our fictionalizing tendencies, our use of distorting artistic models – and that this is a cognitive gain.⁷⁹ Certainly, in the age of narrative imperialism, narrative competence has become a valuable skill. For example, many *literary* narrative devices have become part of our real-life stories and incorporated in our cognitive apparatus without us noticing it. Free indirect discourse, for instance, has been seen in newspaper reporting, and the 'narrative turn' in journalism has led to instances in which journalists describe third-person subjective experiences (based on interviews, inferences from behaviour or mere speculation). Sensitivity to narrative techniques – a skill we refine in reading literature – is a real increase in understanding real-life narratives. Such acuity also helps us to observe and disentangle mythical and rhetorical aspects in stories that surround us and affect our values and behaviour: political speeches, advertisements, entertainment and the like.

Narrative surely is not the only tool in understanding the self, others or the world, and the various meanings and values associated with literature surely do not reduce into narrativity. Still, it is interesting to notice how the focus on narrativity reorients the age-old philosophical debate on the cognitive value of art. Narrative foregrounds, for instance, questions of the processual nature of cognition and the distinctiveness and artificiality of literature, issues of which philosophers have been aware but which they have too often put in the footnotes.

4

Cognition

When studying literature's ability to enlarge our understanding, the focus has traditionally been on the works' mimetic dimension and our imaginative engagement with fiction: literary works are assumed to offer us knowledge of what it is like to be in a certain situation or to see the world from a certain point or points of view, to show us what grief and suffering are, for instance. As of late, it has been fashionable in philosophy, psychology and cognitive literary studies to approach the cognitive value of literature in terms of the *theory of mind*. It is proposed that reading fictional literature is about inferring fictional states of minds and that this activity could improve readers' ability to understand the mental states of others and, perhaps, the workings of the human mind at large. Conversely, philosophers such as Lamarque have argued that literary minds are qualitatively different from real human minds and the mimetic or 'transparent' way of reading literary works does great aesthetic violence to them.

Moreover, the analytic philosophy of art – which has explored the topic for over a half a century – has investigated the cognitive gains of art typically in terms of, or derived from, *truth* and *resemblance*, favouring examples drawn from realist literature. Such an approach seems problematic in, say, modernism where an author ponders, '[W]hat is reality? And who are the judges of reality?'[1] Yet, modernist fiction is characteristically 'epistemological', as the literary critic Brian McHale famously described it. McHale argued that modernist fictions foreground questions such as 'What is there to be known?; Who knows it?; How do they know it, and with what degree of certainty?'[2] Likewise, the critic Alan Palmer thinks that modernist works are 'oriented toward the investigation of such issues as perception and cognition, perspective, the subjective experience of time, and the circulation and reliability of knowledge'.[3] David Herman, yet another critic, maintains that modernist narratives illuminate 'the degree to which perceiving, acting, and thinking are inextricably interlinked, with the constant cross-circulation among these activities accounting for intelligent agents' enactment of a world'.[4] Precisely, the moderns' interest in these fundamental issues, together with the philosophical and psychological erudition of many modernist authors, makes it tempting to approach certain modernist narratives as literary-epistemological explorations.

This chapter examines the assumed cognitive value of literary narratives from the viewpoints of *knowledge, understanding* and *cognitive skills*. Can we learn about the workings of the mind in reading modernist narratives, for instance? If not, could such narratives contribute to cognition some other way which the notion of understanding can capture? Or could literary narratives have value in confounding us and challenging our thinking?

Modernism and knowledge of the mind

Narratology has long celebrated third-person narrators for their ability to give us access to fictional characters' minds. 'Epic fiction is the sole epistemological instance where [. . .] subjectivity [. . .] of a third-person *qua* third-person can be portrayed,' Käte Hamburger proposed in the 1950s.[5] Later, Dorrit Cohn spoke of third-person narrators' 'unnatural power to see into their characters' inner lives,'[6] and Marie-Laure Ryan of narrators' 'supernatural ability of reading into foreign minds'.[7] Likewise, Monika Fludernik states that 'fiction at one point discovers that it [...] can present consciousness extensively as if reading people's minds'.[8]

The epistemic accessibility of fictional minds has later become a subject of dispute in narrative theory, but the idea of the resemblance between real and literary minds and the reader's ability to enter a character's mind remains strong in cognitive literary studies, for instance. The idea that we interpret literary minds like we interpret other people in our everyday encounters is a standard assumption in cognitive approaches to literature.[9] Theory of mind, a psychological concept describing our comprehension of others' minds, has been particularly influential in explaining our engagement with literary narratives. The critic Lisa Zunshine claims that 'ToM makes literature as we know it possible',[10] whereas Gregory Currie proposes that 'mentalizing' (a term he prefers over ToM), the understanding of mental states and the capacity to reason about them, lies at the core of literary interpretation.[11] Alan Palmer, in turn, thinks that 'in essence, narrative is the description of fictional mental functioning'.[12] He claims that '[o]ne of the pleasures of reading novels is the enjoyment of being told what a variety of fictional people are thinking. [...] This is a relief from the business of real life, much of which requires the ability to decode accurately the behavior of others.'[13] Later, Palmer has emphasized the externalist perspective to the mind, yet maintaining that 'readers enter storyworlds primarily by attempting to follow the workings of the fictional minds contained in them'.[14]

It is a commonplace that modernist narratives deal with 'inner experience' and the 'representation of the mind'. Palmer, for instance, claims that 'the modernist novel is still based on a belief in truth and reality' and that modernist authors 'attempt to record as faithfully as possible the workings of fictional minds'.[15] David Herman questions the idea of the *inward turn* in modernism, but asserts that modernist narratives characteristically deal with the representation of the mind:

> [T]he upshot of modernist experimentation was not to plumb psychological depths, but to spread the mind abroad – to suggest that human psychology has the profile it does because of the extent to which it is interwoven with worldly circumstances. The mind does not reside within; instead, it emerges through humans' dynamic interdependencies with the social and material environments they seek to navigate.[16]

Sure enough, modernist literature was greatly affected by developments in modern psychology, such as Ernst Mach's theory of subjective experience, William James's view of the stream of thought or consciousness, Henri Bergson's view of immediate experience and Sigmund Freud's idea of the unconsciousness.[17] Many underline that modern psychology and the modernist movement in literature were intertwined.[18] Moreover, psychological theories were not only an inspiration for authors; for many writers, the exploration of human experience was a programmatic pursuit. In her essay 'Modern Fiction' (1925), Virginia Woolf proposes how writers could come 'closer to life':

> Let us record the atoms as they fall upon the mind in the order in which they fall, let us trace the pattern, however disconnected and incoherent in appearance, which each sight or incident scores upon the consciousness. Let us not take it for granted that life exists more fully in what is commonly thought big than in what is commonly thought small.[19]

In a passage cited ad nauseam, and now once again, Woolf proposes:

> Examine for a moment an ordinary mind on an ordinary day. The mind receives a myriad impressions – trivial, fantastic, evanescent, or engraved with the sharpness of steel. From all sides they come, an incessant shower of innumerable atoms; and as they fall, as they shape themselves into the life of Monday or Tuesday, the accent falls differently from of old; the moment of importance came not here but there; so that, if a writer were a free man and not a slave, if he could write what he chose, not what

he must, if he could base his work upon his own feeling and not upon convention, there would be no plot, no comedy, no tragedy, no love interest or catastrophe in the accepted style, and perhaps not a single button sewn on as the Bond Street tailors would have it. Life is not a series of gig lamps symmetrically arranged; life is a luminous halo, a semi-transparent envelope surrounding us from the beginning of consciousness to the end. Is it not the task of the novelist to convey this varying, this unknown and uncircumscribed spirit, whatever aberration or complexity it may display, with as little mixture of the alien and external as possible? We are not pleading merely for courage and sincerity; we are suggesting that the proper stuff of fiction is a little other than custom would have us believe it.[20]

Referring to Woolf's program, one could defend the mimetic approach and claim that modernism considered itself truer to life and reflected people's experience with their environment; it was the world, or the human character, that had changed. Eric Auerbach, for one, praised Woolf for her talent in capturing the modern epoch.[21] He admires Woolf's *To the Lighthouse* precisely for its lifelikeness and acuity:

[W]hat realistic depth is achieved in every individual occurrence, for example the measuring of the stocking! Aspects of the occurrence come to the fore, and links to other occurrences, which, before this time, had hardly been sensed, which had never been clearly seen and attended to, and yet they are determining factors in our real lives.[22]

There is plenty of genetic evidence available for one who argues that the moderns aimed to give their readers an insight into the human mind. According to her letter, in *Mrs Dalloway* Virginia Woolf intended to 'adumbrate [. . .] a study of insanity & suicide: the world seen by the sane & the insane side by side – something like that'.[23] Many think she succeeded. One critic says that in the work Woolf gives us a 'convincing portrait of schizophrenic breakdown,'[24] whereas another proposes that *Mrs Dalloway*'s passages on Septimus Smith 'allow the reader to experience thoughts, psychological problems, and mental illnesses he or she *does not normally have access to*'.[25] Indeed, it is often suggested that fictional narratives could have such advantages. Monika Fludernik, for one, asserts that fiction 'provides readers with experiences that they cannot have on their own – and this constitutes the fascination of all narratives'.[26] In addition to depicting particular minds, it is repeatedly said that the modernist narratives are particularly well suited to illuminating different ways of conceiving the world. In such a view, the modernist novel is thought of as an epistemological lesson in subjectivism, scepticism or relativism.

Looking for minds in literature is not an odd enterprise. After all, many authors definitely put great effort into the psychological interest (or plausibility) of their works. Then again, we spontaneously look for intentional mindful agency in all sorts of actions and representations, and we are eager to see minds and persons everywhere.[27] We attribute human-like intentions (desires) to non-human animals, such as dogs, and more or less playfully even to plants (a stubborn tree). How about minds in literature? We will run into difficult epistemological problems if we limit ourselves to the mimetic approach. There is, after all, a long way from fictional scenarios, virtual experience and imagination to genuine knowledge of what it is like to be in a certain situation, for example.[28]

Of course, literary works may offer great insights into the human mind, but sometimes an insight may be an impression only. We are also led to the questions of *authority* and *trust*. Perhaps Virginia Woolf is not a real expert on schizophrenia or PTSD or some other sort of mental disorder. Why should we take her as a reliable guide? Moreover, even an author's sincerity, good intentions and thorough research on a topic might not be sufficient for her imaginative depictions to convey knowledge, and an imaginative engagement with a fictional character could furnish the reader with false impressions. James Harold puts the point thus:

> One of the dangers noted in the criticism of William Styron's *Nat Turner* is that white readers would come to believe, falsely, that they had understood *what it had been like* to be a black slave in early nineteenth-century Virginia. This kind of phenomenal knowledge has [. . .] often been thought to be one of the cognitive virtues of literature. But the illusion of phenomenal knowledge can be dangerous epistemically and ethically. If a reader imagines he knows what it is like to be another, then he might attempt to make ethical or policy decisions on that basis. Such decisions could be terrible mistakes, reinforcing racist policies, for example, rather than reforming them. Ignorance and the illusion of knowledge is a dangerous combination.[29]

In addition, the *feeling* of an actual experience in reading a work of fiction ought not lead us to reduce literary interpretation to psychological models. As it has been noted, literary narratives operate on both real-world and literary 'parameters' and have both a mimetic and an artistic dimension; they have a humanly interesting content of which they give an artistic rendering.[30] And it is the latter aspect which sets certain reservations for a straightforward cognitivist approach.[31]

A view from the external perspective

Let us recall the distinction between the internal and the external perspective. Lamarque and Olsen have illustrated how the two perspectives govern our attitude to and speak about fictions. From the internal perspective, we project ourselves into the 'world' of the work and reflect on the characters as *persons*; from the external perspective, we identify them as *fictional characters* and acknowledge their artificiality.[32] In actual literary experience, we assumedly employ both perspectives and shift our focus between them without much noticing it. Still, the distinction is crucial for our understanding of fiction. The perspectives regulate, for instance, the criteria we apply to the characters: from the internal point of view, fictional characters may be 'arrogant' or 'mean', just like real people, whereas from the external perspective, they have properties such as 'being stereotypical' and 'symbolizing the futility of life'.[33] Lamarque claims that

> Although from an internal perspective characters often act and live their lives according to ordinary principles of choice and cause, when viewed, externally, as artefacts in a work of art they become subject to radically different kinds of explanation. Why do they act as they do? Perhaps because they *must* act that way to meet aesthetic, structural and genre-based demands for works of that kind. Perhaps their actions have a symbolic function or a function connected with the development of a theme or because they represent a 'polarity' with another character.[34]

The idea is certainly not limited to that an artistic genre determines the 'logic' or 'rationality' of the story, but that the content of the work is essentially tied to its texture.[35] How do we, for example, identify individual minds in fiction and distinguish between them? Not all cognitive activity is verbal, and we should ask, for instance, whether the narrator depicts thoughts that are already in verbal form in the character's mind or whether the narrator verbalizes the character's perceptions and feelings. And how sincere, or subjective, is the narrator? Characteristic of literature is that these sorts of questions often remain open.

Moreover, (the right sort of) ambiguity in literature is pleasurable. It is fascinating to sense a discrepancy between the narrator and a character, for instance.[36] Dorrit Cohn, for one, remarks that authors like Woolf are 'for some reason unwilling to entrust the presentation of the inner life to the character's own verbal competence'; rather, in *Mrs Dalloway* and *To the Lighthouse* we find searches 'through complicated landscapes of the mind, syntactically too complex to be attributed to inner speech'.[37]

Likewise, the philosopher Lanier Anderson thinks that 'the idiom of Woolf's depiction of Clarissa is elevated – *so* exalted, in fact, that it can occasionally seem unwarranted by the underlying thoughts over which its words are poured'.[38] Further, Anderson illustrates how Woolf's artistic representation transcends our normal cognitive and perceptual frames by making dynamic links between the consciousnesses of the characters:

> Whereas Zunshine highlights a (relatively familiar) phenomenon of 'vertical' integration of mental attitudes that are *about* others' attitudes, and thus take those further attitudes as objects to form a nested hierarchy representing the social situation (form: Richard sees that Lady Bruton knows that Miss Brush thinks that Hugh's beliefs about the sentiments of the *Times* editors are bunkum), by contrast, what is demanded in the jaunt around London is a facility for navigating 'horizontal' connections joining the thoughts of one person to those of another so as to permit the smooth flow of consciousness across different minds. Such horizontal connections are unfamiliar from everyday life. After all, the possibility of consciously transitioning from one person's thought to another's *in real life* (as opposed to in the fictional world) would seem to depend on the truth of something like Clarissa's implausible thesis that consciousness can extend from one mind into another, flowing across the juncture created by common attention.[39]

Nevertheless, Anderson remarks that 'horizontal mental linkage is not a feature of ordinary social existence, so its mastery will not build up our socially useful "Machiavellian intelligence"'.[40] This leads us to a further point, namely, that literary minds are products of textual artifice and appreciated partly for their artificiality. Lamarque asserts that

> The whole modernist movement in art amounted to a challenge at a fundamental level to the idea of representing reality. At its best

modernism exhibited the plurality of worlds, private and public, in contrast to some single 'objective' world given in experience. Once representation itself had been exposed as a kind of artifice it was natural for artists to highlight the artifice of their own media.[41]

If we abandon the mimetic approach to literary cognition, is there anything left? Could literary narratives enhance cognition after we acknowledge their artificiality and the dissimilarities between real-world and literary experiences? Is there value in literary narratives deviating from the natural norms?

Beyond knowledge

Analytical philosophical problems regarding the epistemology of art are, however, partly self-inflicted and have arisen as the result of philosophers' conceiving of knowledge in a frame of comparative narrowness. As analytic philosophers have identified knowledge (mostly) with propositional knowledge and focused on assertions and the referential use of language, the status of art has been problematic. Philosophers have found it difficult to explain the value, seriousness or significance of artworks without referring to truth or terms related to truth. On the other hand, cognitivists have formulated alternative epistemic notions in explaining the value of art. Theodore M. Greene, for instance, argued in the 1930s and 1940s for the cognitive value of art in terms of 'artistic truth'.[42] One of his critics, W. T. Stace, dismissed such an epistemic oddity outright:

> My view is that there is only one kind of truth, which consists in the correct ascription of a predicate or relation to a subject. Accordingly, every artistic truth is or contains a judgment. If this is not the case, then there is no justification for calling it 'truth'. *It may be, for all I know, something very valuable, something perhaps even*

> more precious than truth. But truth it can not be, for only that which is capable of being expressed as a judgment can be true or false.[43]

As the passage shows, a philosopher may concede a high value to art – 'something perhaps even more precious than truth' – and yet mistrust its *epistemic* value.[44] Moreover, it is characteristic of the debate that there are two divergent notions of 'cognition' employed in it. Dorothy Walsh nicely summarized the two opposing intuitions in the 1940s:

> The arts have customarily been regarded as sources of intellectual nourishment. They have been accepted as *vehicles of insight, revelation, and enlarged comprehension*. Dissenting voices have, however, been raised from time to time, voices which express with indignation a denial of the value of art as a means to *any adequate knowledge*.[45]

Cognitivists typically, but not always, rely on non-orthodox concepts of truth, such as 'insight', 'revelation' and 'enlarged comprehension' – or 'artistic truth', 'poetic truth' and 'literary truth'. Most cognitivists maintain that artistic truths cannot be comprehensively expressed in propositions.[46] Many 'anticognitivists', by contrast, are willing to admit that works of literature may 'broaden our horizons', give us insights or inspire our thinking, but they simply maintain that the works do not furnish us with truth and knowledge with which they equate cognitive value. The debate is thus not about the significance of literature itself but the epistemic term used in describing that significance. The literary critic Charles Altieri insightfully acknowledges both the cognitivist and anti-cognitivist intuitions in saying that

> literature seems too important to culture not to be seen as conveying some kind of knowledge, yet if we put too much analytic pressure on the forms of representation literature offers, we may well lose its special qualities and treat it only as inferior social science, psychology, or philosophy.[47]

Likewise, the literary scholar Michael Wood suggests what particular forms of knowledge may taste like: 'the knowledge of the very gap between knowledge and life, between what can be said and what can't; of what takes the place of thinking when we encounter or engineer the unthinkable; of an array of scarcely nameable forms of loss and regret'; nonetheless, he wonders 'whether knowledge is the right word for what we keep meeting in literature'.[48]

In contemporary aesthetics, non-orthodox forms of cognition – artistic 'insight', 'revelation' or 'enlargened comprehension' – have mostly been approached in terms of understanding.[49] The notion of understanding draws from nineteenth-century discussions on the differences between the humanities and the sciences – Wilhelm Dilthey's view of *Verstehen*, most notably. It has travelled to analytic epistemology and from there to aesthetics, via philosophy of science and the study of scientific explanation. As remarked in Chapter 3, the distinction between knowledge and understanding has recently received interest in epistemology in the analytic tradition, and analytic epistemologists have started to explore understanding as a cognitive achievement of its own kind.

Several epistemologists have argued that the goal of our epistemic enterprises is not knowledge but understanding. We can, for instance, know something without understanding it, as the philosophers Christoph Baumberger, Claus Beisbart and Georg Brun remark.[50] Catherine Elgin, in turn, states that understanding should be a central epistemological concern and that it is needed to explain why knowledge is valuable.[51] Some epistemologists have made references to the history of philosophy, maintaining that the Greek word *episteme* denoted what we now call understanding – 'roughly, the good of being able to "grasp" or "see" how the various parts of the world were systematically related', as Stephen Grimm puts it[52] – and arguing that epistemology ought to study understanding.

Conceptual enhancement and revision

Many contemporary aestheticians argue that the cognitive value of literature is not primarily in the works supplying new knowledge to readers but advancing readers' comprehension.[53] The theories often make use of the term 'understanding', although typically as a non-technical term or without committing to a particular epistemology of understanding. These theories state, roughly put, that the cognitive value of literature lies in the works 'advancing' or 'clarifying' readers' understanding of things they already know,[54] 'enhancing', 'enlarging' or 'enriching' their existing knowledge;[55] or helping them to 'acknowledge' things, to see concepts contextualized in 'concrete forms of human engagement'.[56]

David Novitz, for instance, thinks that literary works might help us to notice conceptual relationships we have not thought of before, for example, to become aware of the relationship between pride and self-deception which would lead the readers to 'rearrange' or 'remodel' their world.[57] In turn, in his theory of 'clarificationism', Noël Carroll maintains that works of art may deepen their readers' moral understanding by rehearsing the readers' moral knowledge and emotions.[58] He thinks that in interpreting a (narrative) work, readers access and mobilize their cognitive, emotive and moral repertoire, and in applying and engaging this repertoire, they may come to explore and augment it. A literary work thus becomes an 'occasion for exercising knowledge, concepts, and emotions that [readers] have already, in one sense, learned'.[59] Carroll suggests that

> In the course of engaging a given narrative we may need to reorganize the hierarchical orderings of our moral categories and premises, or to reinterpret those categories and premises in the light of new paradigm instances and hard cases, or to reclassify barely acknowledged phenomena afresh – something we might be

provoked to do by a feminist author who is able to show us injustice where before all we saw was culture as usual.⁶⁰

One of Carroll's examples is Lorraine Hansberry's play *A Raisin in the Sun* (1959), which he takes to provide a possibility for white audiences to 'deepen' their understanding of the principle that all people should be treated equally no matter what colour they are.⁶¹

The idea of conceptual enhancement is based on a familiar aspect of our encounter with literature. We read literary works, among other reasons, in order to understand and clarify our conceptions, whatever they are. Perhaps we do not gain much new knowledge in terms of propositions; rather, the detailed representation that is characteristic of literary works helps us to give expression to our existing but inarticulate conceptions. However, the idea of conceptual enhancement often includes the idea that literary works may revise our conceptions and values. Novitz, for one, claims that literary works may 'offer radically new ways of thinking about or perceiving aspects of our environment' and 'enable us to see old and familiar objects in a radically different light'.⁶² Catherine Wilson, in turn, states that '[a] person may learn from a novel [. . .] if he is forced to revise or modify, e.g. his concept of "reasonable action" through a recognition of an alternative as presented in the novel'.⁶³ Like clarifying our existing views, literary works may also provide us alternative ways of thinking and perceiving. Of course, as literary works of a fictional kind fall short of *justifying* the views they promote, their ability to revise our conceptions is weak and depends on our willingness to learn and change.

A somewhat related view in psychology and cognitive literary studies makes use of the terms 'frames', 'scripts' and 'parameters'. In arguing for the value of stories in constructing reality, the psychologist Jerome Bruner proposes that

> The innovative storyteller [. . .] may go beyond the conventional scripts, leading people to see human happenings in a fresh way,

indeed, in a way they had never before 'noticed' or even dreamed. The shift from Hesiod to Homer, the advent of 'inner adventure' in Laurence Sterne's *Tristram Shandy*, the advent of Flaubert's perspectivalism, or Joyce's epiphanizing of banalities – these are all innovations that probably shaped our narrative versions of everyday reality as well as changed the course of literary history, the two perhaps being not that different.[64]

The view that literary narratives could enrich our cognitive frames or scripts has become popular in cognitive narratology. Monika Fludernik, for one, maintains that through repeated use, 'non-natural narrational frames' become 'naturalized'; second-person narration and a dying person's interior monologue, for example, have lost their 'surprise factor' and become 'natural frames', part of our cognitive stock.[65] Some think further that the new frames that literary works have on offer may be valuable for our thought. Jan Alber, for instance, claims that 'one should study literary fiction because it allows us to transcend ourselves and to experience scenarios and situations which are strictly speaking impossible in the real world'.[66] Of Alber's particular interest are 'unnatural' scenarios and events, which 'significantly widen the cognitive horizon of human awareness; they challenge our limited perspective on the world and invite us to address questions that we do not normally address'.[67] Alber maintains that literary narratives could generate *new* cognitive frames by blending scripts (animals, corpses or inanimate objects as narrators)[68] or *enrich* our existing frames by stretching them 'beyond real-world possibilities until the parameters include the strange phenomena with which we are confronted'.[69] In addition to providing readers new frames and enhancing their existing frames, Alber thinks that the 'unnatural scenarios of literary fiction are particularly well designed to *make us more open and more flexible* because they urge us to deal with radical forms of otherness or strangeness'.[70] According to him, openness and flexibility of imagination characteristically link to growth in ethical understanding (tolerance).

Philosophical theories of conceptual enhancement typically highlight works that support our existing views about life. What if, for example, some of our conceptions are misguided and the works actually strengthen these misconceptions? Or what if the new frames we gain from art are potentially harmful? If there is a possibility for change, is not there also a possibility for things to get worse; if certain literary works can improve our understanding, surely some others may harm it?[71]

Another worry in the enhancement view is the ambiguity and complexity of literary representations. Literary works may surely clarify or revise our understanding of various things, but how are we to determine what is, exactly, the 'new view' we should adopt? Traditionally, non-propositional cognitivist theories have maintained that literary works represent lifelike and detailed situations and thus reveal their ethical complexity. For example, Martha Nussbaum famously praises the 'variety and indeterminacy' of a good fiction in moral philosophical enquiry.[72] She thinks that by revealing the 'mystery and indeterminacy of "our actual adventure"', literary works 'characterize life more richly and truly' than philosophical examples.[73] Although a reader's bewilderment with a literary work is acknowledged in the discussion of the cognitive and ethical value of literature, and even praised as a literary-philosophical merit, the phenomenon is typically ignored in favour of edification and clarification, or truths and knowledge as the ultimate end. Cognitivists often celebrate literary works for their ambiguity and indeterminacy, but they seldom pursue this claim seriously, for example, by recognizing different ways by which the 'cognitively valuable' content of a work could be rendered. Instead, the theories tend to promote or imply objectivism which nullifies the complexity.[74]

But great works of art do not let us off easily. As Milan Kundera puts it, '[e]very novel says to the reader: "Things are not as simple as you think."'[75] Indeed, literary works such as novels characteristically have intricate structures and they allow for, call for, different viewpoints to their content. Moreover, significant works of literature tend to be reread, and at different times readers are likely to construe their content – including the 'insights' – differently, for their interests in the content change with their situation.[76] The idea that the content of a literary work and conceptions it promotes may be interpreted in various ways is a commonplace in literary culture. As Lamarque puts it, 'one of the pleasures of a literary reading is to notice different ways that the content can be imaginatively construed.'[77]

It would be rather odd to hold that complexity and ambiguity[78] are aesthetic values – a view which I take for granted – and simultaneously maintain that literary works provide us mere simple truths or enhance or clarify our existing conceptions or provide us new clear-cut frames. Because of their complexity, literary works may also confound us, as in allowing for multiple equally plausible interpretations.[79] Richard Posner asks, 'What moral guidance does *The Golden Bowl* offer its readers?', and answers that

> It seems to invite a variety of incompatible moral responses. One can side with the adulterers, finding Maggie the insufferable rich girl from start to finish and thinking it wrong that Charlotte should lose out to her merely because Maggie is rich and Charlotte poor. One can look upon the prince as a golddigger (for it is plain that he married Maggie for her money, his excuse being that his aristocratic status obligates him to support his relatives in Italy) and think Maggie poor-spirited both for marrying him in the first place and for condoning his adultery.[80]

Posner argues that these interpretations of the work may coexist happily, for '*The Golden Bowl* is richly ambiguous and exerts no pressure on the reader to select the one "right" reading.'[81] Elsewhere, he remarks that

> Works of literature that we deem great tend to be open-ended; that is a condition for their surviving cultural change and becoming

canonized. These works are something of a Rorschach test. People obsessed with politics, with what they think is social justice, with contemporary social problems generally, or with historical injustices (such as the mistreatment of Jews by Christians or blacks by whites) may find it a psychological impossibility to divorce the experience of reading literature from their nonliterary concerns.[82]

Initially fascinated with ambiguity, proponents of the enhancement view tend to explain perplexity and confusion away from literary experience and, in the end, construe literary works as illustrations for a principle or proposition. They are uncomfortable with works that leave us with bewilderment and doubt, which is no wonder, if it is truth and knowledge that we are after – and especially if there is a possibility that literary works could confuse our moral reasoning. While I am sympathetic to the idea that literary works may clarify and revise our conceptions, I think that conceptual *confusion* related to literary cognition has to be examined a bit further.[83] I do not mean the turn towards confusion as a cheap, mystifying move; rather, I am worried about the gap between 'literary' and philosophical ways of reading.

Complexity and confusion

In philosophical aesthetics, debate on the cognitive value of literature has traditionally focused on the end product of literary interpretation and attempted to capture it in terms of *truth* and *knowledge*. The study on the cognitive value of literature should not, however, be limited to debating the truths and knowledge which literary works might provide but should also acknowledge the procedural dimension, the reader's journey to understanding. Moreover, while literary works assumedly may give us propositional and non-propositional knowledge and enhance, clarify and revise our conceptual knowledge, the works may also confuse us and make us doubt what to think and, further, the confusion thus caused may have cognitive value of a significant kind.

In the Western culture, cognition has been associated with vision, clarity and light. Nonetheless, there is a long-standing tradition of considering literature and art in general as the nocturnal side of thought. This view manifested itself most prominently in German romanticism and is nowadays often associated with the post-structuralist thought and figures such as Kristeva, Blanchot and Derrida.[84] In more modest analytic variations of the view, it has been suggested that literature could show the limitations of rational thinking and perhaps supplement it. There have been attempts to describe this cognitive and ethical function of literature using negative terms such as 'disturbance', 'obscurity' and 'confusion'.

For instance, Bernard Harrison argues that literary works *challenge* and *disrupt* our thinking. In Harrison's view, the cognitive gains of literature are in the first place gains in self-knowledge and as such 'of an essentially negative kind'.[85] As he sees it, literary works

> disturb the self in its natural but mistaken conviction that the terms in which it habitually construes the world are the only terms in which the world is capable of being construed, simply by displacing the language, the system of connections and differences between terms which articulates and constitutes that habitual way of looking at things.[86]

For Harrison, the value of literature is 'its power to act as a standing rebuke and irritant to the dominant paradigm of knowledge',[87] whereas the knowledge it provides 'is knowledge of limits and of limitations: ours'.[88] In a similar vein, Eileen John proposes that rather than supplying new ways of thinking, literary works sometimes 'lead us to places of obscurity or untested areas in entrenched ways of thinking'.[89] Further, she thinks that in such cases, 'the work provides a context in which we can think fruitfully about the conceptual issues raised, where the line of inquiry we pursue is integrated into our efforts to judge the characters and events'.[90] John also distinguishes her survey from earlier approaches which credit the author (or the work) for presenting the audience new conceptions, and argues that the conceptual knowledge gained from a literary work should be seen as a result of the reader's interpretative activity. As her example, she uses Grace Paley's short story 'Wants' (1974), which tells of an encounter of a divorced couple and which she finds conceptually challenging. In discussing the story, John pays attention to the ex-husband's use of the word 'want' when he tells the ex-wife that she 'didn't want anything' and will 'always want nothing'. John remarks that in these sentences, 'wanting' can be understood as both desiring and lacking:

> Although it is fairly clear that the ex-husband is thinking of her as desiring nothing, the reader is left to wonder which meaning is most appropriate and, I think, is likely to feel confused about how distinct the two meanings are. We think about *lack* shading into *need*, and *need* shading into *desire*, and perhaps we compare the negative, inert connotation of want-as-lack to the somehow forward-looking connotation of want-as-desire.[91]

In John's view, 'the ex-husband and the narrator each use different senses of the term "want," and thereby summon up different networks of associated concepts'.[92] And because of the confusion caused by these characters' different uses of the term, John thinks that the story makes the reader explore the nature of the concept of wanting.

David Novitz, in turn, asserts that fiction 'often explores, teases, and tests our moral standards and attitudes'.[93] He argues that much of what we consider we learn from fiction does not square with our established beliefs; rather, fiction 'flouts, fragments, and disturbs them – and yet we have little doubt that we have learned something useful from the fiction'.[94] Similarly, Elgin proposes that

[a]rt [. . .] challenges complacent assumptions, not just about matters of fact, but also about how problems and proposed solutions should be framed. It pushes the boundaries, reconfigures domains, highlights unusual perspectives and stances. It thus leads us into terra incognita, where the route to cognitive advancement is nowhere clearly marked. It does not, and does not purport to deliver literal, descriptive truths. It seeks, rather, to challenge, to disorient, to disrupt, to explore and thereby to reveal what more regimented approaches lack the resources to attempt.[95]

The critic Colin Davis, for his part, argues that the ethical value of literature, or its contribution to our reflection on ethical matters, is not as much in the works realizing and refining our moral values as in obstructing and confusing our thoughts about them. Davis examines the ethical complexity of Albert Camus's short story 'L'Hôte' (1957, 'The Guest'), which describes an encounter with a French Algerian schoolteacher and an Arab, who is said to have committed a murder. In the story, the schoolteacher is forced to deliver the Arab to the authorities; however, he allows the Arab to choose whether to go to prison or escape. Not knowing that the Arab chose to go to prison, his brothers leave the schoolteacher a message in which they threaten to kill him for handing their brother to the authorities. The story is extremely complex, starting with the title which can be translated as either 'The Host' or 'The Guest', and which can refer either to the schoolteacher (host for the Arab, and a *French* Algerian) or to the Arab (guest of the schoolteacher, and an *Algerian*). After introducing different ethical perspectives that critics have taken on the story content and examining its ambiguity, Davis concludes that the story 'stubbornly withholds the sort of information and insight which would allow us confidently to pin down its political and ethical positions'.[96] He argues that works such as Camus's short story 'provoke and intrigue because they withhold their answers, not because they make them available to the properly attentive reader'.[97] In Davis's view,

> The reluctance to deliver clear messages and conclusions may be Camus's, or it may be something which inheres in literature itself. What is most important is that a sense of perplexity belongs to the experience of reading and as such it is ethically valuable.[98]

A cognitivist theory should take these points seriously. Literary works may contribute to our thinking by triggering conceptual enquiries of substantial kind; yet they might do this in a sense negatively, so that the 'outcome' is more of a doubt than an insight: although the stories call for ethical reflection and represent ethical decision making, for instance, they escape our attempts to draw conclusions from them.[99] Also, we are generally fascinated by artworks that perplex us and value such works for obstructing straightforward interpretations.

The idea that the experience of confusion could have real cognitive benefits may sound strange in rationalist (or 'heliotropic'[100]) philosophy that is after illumination and clear and distinct ideas. For instance, while Davis's characterization of literary experiences is fascinating, it may be difficult to see how confusion, that is, uncertainty or bewilderment, could be cognitively valuable. After all, perplexity is not something we strive for in our cognitive enterprises, neither is confusion a desirable outcome of, say, moral reasoning. Indeed, from a cognitive point of view, confusion is an unpleasant mental state. A confused mind is not likely to think or act well. How, then, could literary works that obstruct our thinking be cognitively valuable, assuming that human beings ultimately aim for knowledge and truth, or advancing their understanding?

The value of confusion

There seems to be a difference between the feeling of confusion in practical life and in literary experience. Roughly put, moral confusion in real life is unpleasant, when it involves one in decision making or when the decisions somehow affect one's life: when one needs to take action or when something real is at stake. Encountering confusing events fictionally is, however, different: interactive fiction put aside, the reader of a literary work is following the dramatic events typically in the role of an observer. Literature provides us a relatively safe area to be perplexed and to put our beliefs and conceptions into test.

Moreover, there are various kinds of confusion associated with literary experience, and of these, not all are interesting as for the cognitive value of literature.[101] It is difficult to see the value of confusion caused by obscurity that is not motivated in any way but just to give an impression of profoundness. Confusion, in order to affect the reader's reflections and be valuable, needs to be somehow intelligibly or aesthetically justified and intriguing. There has to be some sort of coherence or continuity or unity – or a reason to disturb them – so that the reader may engage and proceed with a work that confounds her. Moreover, different literary genres also allow different kinds of indeterminacy – for the individual works to toy with.[102] For example, perplexity caused by a character's inconsistent or irrational behaviour in the existential novel has a motivation: a world that just is not meaningful. In turn, the perplexity caused by the multiplicity of meaning, the uncertainty of the speaker of a work and other perplexities stemming from the structure of a work are fascinating characteristics of the modernist novel.[103] Whether perplexity is intriguing depends on several matters and can perhaps only be evaluated case-by-case. In general terms, the sort of confusion that is interesting from a cognitivist point of view takes place when the reader's beliefs and principles, such as her conception of 'reasonable action', prove unsuccessful in construing the story or its elements in a meaningful way.

How can even such confusion contribute to cognition? First of all, it wakes one up and reminds one that things are not as simple as one has thought. It leads to understanding that we tend to resort to simplifications, conventions and dogmatic thinking, and it tells us that we should be vary of such dispositions, to remember the difference between the abstract model and life. Actually, there has been a tradition of avoiding literary examples in Anglo-American moral philosophy, for literary works have been seen to 'introduce an unnecessary complexity into one's philosophizing'[104] and confuse the philosophers who try to look coolly at 'the logical issues involved'.[105] However, after the 'literary turn' in Anglo-American moral philosophy, many philosophers have argued that the confusion we encounter in trying to make sense of a complex and detailed moral dilemma in literature assists us to comprehend the philosophical issues at hand 'more fully'. Literature is said not to depict solutions but to aid us in 'the imaginative recreation of moral perplexities'[106] and to help us to notice their salient features, that is, which factors are important in ethical reflection.[107]

Berys Gaut, for one, claims that by getting us to imagine vividly, a fiction 'shows us what some of our deepest commitments are, and how they are apparently inconsistent with a general principle that we might otherwise have found attractive'.[108] While the story which Gaut refers to in speaking of general principles – that is, Bernard Williams's philosophical thought-experiment of a person able to save a group of Indians by accepting to shoot one of them – might show a reader that she *cannot* kill one of the Indians (and for that reasons, all of the Indians will be shot), it only shows the maxim impossible to follow (or utilitarian calculus alone insufficient for moral choices). Although Williams's fiction contributes to philosophical discourse, by illustrating that personal commitments cannot be overridden in a way that utilitarianism does, it does not provide a pleasant resolution or answer.

When a work seems to offer us explicit or implicit assertions or promote a given view, we can often simply accept or reject those assertions or views.[109] Confusion, in turn, encourages us to seek answers and to ask questions. When encountering fictional problems, we yearn for resolution – a promise for it is embodied in the concept of drama. But as noted, many works resist attempts to find solutions for the questions they provoke. Our urge to find a solution for a dilemma or an unpleasant complex situation triggers thought-processes and ideally stimulates cognitive skills. Confusion makes us test and revise our conceptual resources. If our conceptual resources prove insufficient in explaining a given phenomenon, the resources might be reassessed. Although confusion may be a phase on the way to clarity – before getting back to our existing beliefs or adopting new ones – it does not need to lead to refinement and reorganization in order to be valuable. The procedure, whether it leads to conceptual revision or not, is already significant, as we notice the complexity of a situation, become aware of our conceptual restrictions and are encouraged to seek answers. Confusion caused by a literary work might also lead to, assumedly temporal, conceptual distortion or uncertainty of our beliefs and principles, or even disbelief in rationality. After all, obscurity may also be used as a rhetorical device to spread falsehoods or mislead the hearer, as Aristotle remarked.[110] But conceptual revision can take place only if the reader is willing to adopt new conceptions or to give perplexity a change.

Confusion and literary interpretation

Philosophers in the anti-cognitivist camp have suggested that the conceptual activity which takes place in literary interpretation hardly affects the reader's actual conceptions. For instance, Lamarque and Olsen claim that a literary work provides concepts 'its own alternative realm of application'; it offers 'an imaginative rather than a discursive interpretation of the concepts'.[111] It is open to dispute whether the bewilderment which a reader experiences in trying to understand fictional events carries outside the fictional world and affects her understanding of reality. In other words, it is one thing to say that literary interpretation requires conceptual adjustment and quite another thing to say that this contributes to the reader's knowledge and thinking in general. Indeed, it has been argued that cognitivist theories do not establish a distinction between a reader *recognizing* a conception in a work and actually *adopting* it.[112]

In this question, I basically side with Eileen John who, referring to 'the general nature of concepts', argues that concepts 'are tools to be applied consistently in every context'.[113] John remarks pragmatically that her confidence in the belief that concepts (terms) have the same sense in reality and fiction comes from the fact that she is 'able to think constructively about how to articulate the issues of the content, domain, and point of the desire concept as they are raised in the story'.[114] We might apply the notion of 'minimal departure' to the use of terms in literature too: we begin reading a literary work with an understanding of the standard senses of a term, and if we notice that a term is used in a deviant sense in the work, we try to adopt that new sense. If we maintain that concepts are general in their nature and a fiction may provide a concept a new sense – or illustrate novel connections between two concepts – we are led to admit that it is possible for a literary work to alter our conceptual apparatus as a part of a literary-fictional engagement with the work. Whether this actually happens is an issue to be explored in the chapter on evidence.

I am, however, happy to admit that the cognitive gains of a literary work are, in the end, a product of a collaboration with the work and the reader. Moreover, one could expect that the gains partly depend on a reader's interests, her literary and cognitive skills, her current situation and the like. Also, one might assume that readers differ in how they respond to perplexing narratives and, say, whether they take the role of an empathetic participant or a critical observer when encountering moral dilemmas in literature. Nevertheless, it is worth noting that academic critics and other professional readers also get confused. For academic critics, Marguerite Duras's works are not simply puzzles to be solved and given a determine meaning.

It is another matter though to what sort of *activity* the experience of confusion leads a particular reader: trying to comprehend the story, – an act in which the assumed conceptual changes are likely to happen, in a sense, in the background – or to explicit reflection on abstract concepts. Anticognitivists who hold an autonomous view of literature argue that if a reader ultimately learns something from a narrative, it is 'only' triggered by the work and gained by contingent *extra-literary*, philosophical reflection. Perhaps. But without the work, there might not have been the stimulus. Literature was needed for the scales to fall from the reader's eyes, to encourage her to look for answers.

As confusion, that is, not comprehending, is generally an unpleasant state, it is open to question if readers tend to avoid it in their interpretations and compel a meaning to a story. Moreover, understanding the ambiguity of a work requires critical or interpretive skills. Perhaps the more the reader has literary competence, the more she is able to find conflict in the work. For an individual who is comfortable with uncertainty, fictions have much to give. If there is something that fiction can 'teach' us, it is that ultimately we do not know. Leila Haaparanta, for one, has defended an agnostic attitude towards empathetic knowledge as a condition of it. She argues that an empathic person doubts her capacity to know the other's emotions and admits that her knowledge is abstract; empathy requires one to admit the limits of one's knowledge and to respect the other as other.[115] Such a view on empathy is very interesting with regard to fiction. Perhaps the cognitive value of literature, or an important dimension of it, lies in its challenging us and showing our limitations.

Understanding: *pro et contra*

The shift from knowledge to understanding encapsulates many popular conceptions about the value of literature, and the view has a good deal of appeal. For example, our inability to draw 'messages' out of literary works is not a problem but part of the value of literature: rather than providing answers, literary works provoke questions and prompt us to explore solutions for them. Because of their complexity, literary works often escape our attempts to formulate theses out of their content; yet, we sense that the works are at about something very important.

The concept of understanding allows us to go beyond realistic representation, verisimilitude and knowledge narrowly conceived. Extreme or 'unnatural' fictional characters might help us to understand *abstract concepts*, for instance.[116] Moreover, in preferring understanding to true beliefs, we can attach cognitive value even to *false* views that literary works express or convey (we come to comprehend – yet not to accept – *distorted*, for example, immoral, viewpoints).[117] Cognitivism based on the notion of understanding could account for the value of a wide variety of cultural artefacts, such as propagandistic works which help us to learn about persuasion and human psychology, for instance. Moreover, the processual epistemology behind understanding-based cognitivism – that is, the view that literary works trigger cognitive processes and that understanding comes in degrees – is absorbing and intuitively plausible. It could be used in partly explaining, from a cognitive point of view, why people return to works they consider important and why they render the works' content differently in different times.

Many anticognitivists are happy to grant that literary works may provide their readers with new perspectives on familiar things, refine the readers' perception and offer them new categories for classifying objects – these are commonplaces in literary culture. Of course artworks 'broaden our horizons', they admit. But from an epistemic point of view, the anticognitivists argue, notions such as 'enhanced understanding' and 'enriched knowledge' depart too far from the standard notions of truth and knowledge and obfuscate rather than clarify the matter. Thus W. T. Stace says that 'if the esthetician insists on claiming for art a separate and peculiar kind of truth, inaccessible to the common conceptual "intellect", he will in the end achieve nothing except to bring ridicule upon his branch of philosophy'.[118] Similarly, Hilary Putnam argues that if the cognitivist's claim of the existence of artistic knowledge as 'knowledge of man' additionally maintains that this knowledge is more important than scientific knowledge, 'we have a full-blown obscurantist position – not the position of the serious student or critic of literature [. . .] but the position of the religion of literature'.[119] Jerome Stolnitz, for his part, calls cognitivists' ideas of artistic truth 'vague' and 'quite gaseous'.[120] Lamarque says that in spelling out the cognitive payoff of literature, cognitivists often resort to metaphors,[121] which are not typically considered sufficiently explanatory in analytic philosophy. And Roger Pouivet, while defending art's cognitive value, thinks that Goodman's view of art as *worldmaking* is simply exaggerated:

> The world I step into when I leave the Centre Georges Pompidou is the same vale of tears I quitted before entering the building to see an exhibition. To say that the world has changed is just a way of saying that I have been impressed; it is not a genuinely ontological remark.[122]

The idea that literary narratives could widen our 'mental universe'[123] or even 'the cognitive horizon of human awareness'[124] is sympathetic. Nonetheless, it is far from clear *how* our gaining new or enhanced cognitive frames from literary works actually enriches our understanding of our life-world. How does our engagement with Clarissa Dalloway's perfectly unnatural 'extended mind', for instance, improve our social cognition? The same requirement goes for the idea of 'imaginative stretching'. Imagining logical impossibilities is great intellectual fun – as in Borges's stories, for instance – but what do we 'gain', so to say, from imagining them? The idea of imaginative flexibility and ethical openness is nice, but optimistic. Behind these views is the familiar idea of *defamiliarization*, the technique of presenting to audiences common things in an unfamiliar or strange way in order to enhance their perception of the familiar. In this thought, artworks distance us from the familiar and make us reflect upon it with new eyes.

However, the mere repetition of these cognitivist ideas leads us into the danger of establishing a *religion* of literature, and from a dull philosophical perspective, the claims have begun to look like dogmas. Again, it is unclear whether literary works *actually* produce changes such as those described earlier. And to repeat: while the comprehension of a literary work often requires us to adjust or modify our cognitive apparatus, to 'blend schemes', for example, it is unknown if the conceptual modifications required in the interpretation of the work carry over the literary experience and affect the reader's actual cognitive mechanisms. The matter is extremely difficult to study; yet, some evidence for the cognitivist's claims is needed. How could we have even *some* support for the assertion of such changes *commonly* taking place as a result of a *literary* response? This is a real worry; as noted, the claims are problematic also because they imply that all conceptual changes would automatically be for the good – which they clearly are not.[125] What if *Mrs Dalloway* rather distorts than enhances our understanding of reality?

5

Evidence

Recently, many of those who are sceptical about the cognitive benefits of literature have called for methodological discussion and demanded evidence for the claim that readers actually learn from literature. As noted, the cognitivist's disregard of evidence is problematic also because she tends to limit herself to praising the alleged beneficial effects of literature and typically simply neglects the possibility that some literary works might have a negative effect on the reader. This chapter explores issues that have been paid too little attention in the debate: the *evidence* that cognitivist theories provide for their claims and the *methods* used in studying learning from literature.

The question of evidence is complicated when it comes to cognitivist theories based on unorthodox epistemological notions, such as the concept of understanding. The problem is that in describing the cognitive value of literature in terms of advancing the reader's understanding, it is very difficult to find articulations of those benefits, for the concept implies that they are ultimately non-propositional and possibly inarticulate; yet, the cognitivist has to provide some evidence for her claims. After all, the oldest trick in the book is to defend the cognitive gains of art by asserting that they are beyond propositions and thus inexpressible. Lamarque wisely asks,

> how is this 'illumination' or 'enhanced' understanding manifested? Would we expect that those immersed in the great works of literature understand people and the world better than those

who are not so well read? Yet there seems no evidence that such readers are especially knowledgeable about human traits, as are psychologists or social scientists or even philosophers.[1]

Moreover, the parties to the debate are not in agreement about what counts as evidence of such changes. A look at different notions of justification is thus in place.

The armchair

Appeals to intuition and introspection as evidence have traditionally been central in analytic philosophy. In the philosophy of literature, the philosopher often illuminates the assumed perlocutionary effect of a given work by describing her personal experience with it; others are expected to react to the work the way the philosopher does. Moreover, the philosopher's interpretations can be, at least partly, *normative*: the philosopher can support her theoretical claims by showing that the interpretation she proposes is possible and rewarding – and ideally better than its rivals.[2]

When it comes to the cognitive value of literature, it is thought that the philosopher's task is to show, by pointing to particular works, what kind of things readers *can* learn from literature and help others to see those features. For example, when arguing that empathy is integral to literary appreciation, Susan Feagin says that in reading a passage on Mr Ramsay (in Woolf's *To the Lighthouse*), 'I *feel* his vulnerability, his emptiness and loss, as it is evoked by this passage and also how important Mrs Ramsay was as his source of security'.[3] Jenefer Robinson, in turn, says that 'If I am merely reporting my emotional experience, then I am not making any claims about what anyone else should experience on reading the work, but if I am offering "an interpretation", then presumably I want other people to endorse it too'.[4] On the other hand, the anti-cognitivist may question the proposed interpretation. She may further state that she has not herself recognized any conceptual or whatsoever improvement as a result of reading the work. She may claim that in reading the work she is offered a perspective towards the fictional content of the work but that taking that perspective does not amount to learning or change of any sort.

Gregory Currie has expressed doubts about the traditional armchair method in philosophical aesthetics. He points out that *intuition* has been shown to be a fallible source of knowledge and that philosophers' intuitions might not be widely shared outside academia.[5] Further, our *imaginings* are not a good guide to what we would actually do in a given hypothetical situation, for it seems that minor contextual matters affect our attitudes and behaviour; thus, we ought not to put much weight on the value of fiction in teaching us about ourselves.[6] *Introspection* cannot be trusted either, for our metacognition is biased and governed by irrational principles.[7] Moreover, Currie argues that cognitivists' claims of the educative function of the works 'are all empirical claims with no self-validating power' and that the educative function 'cannot be known in advance of seeing what sorts of behavioural changes exposure to the narrative in question leads to'.[8]

Currie's demand for empirical evidence points to a blind spot in the discussion. Nonetheless, one has to be careful in interpreting the cognitivist's claims. To begin with, there are roughly two different, although partly intertwined, philosophical projects interested in literature: first, the project which seeks to use literary works in philosophical enquiry and which has been prominent especially in moral philosophy and, second, the project which aims to explain the cognitive value of literature in general. Of these, the former project does not attempt to describe the practice of literature and cannot thus be accused of the lack of empirical evidence. Moreover, it is not always clear whether a philosopher's claims in the second project are descriptive or prescriptive; empirical-looking claims about general readers may be rhetorical persuasion.[9] As for their normativity, one may of course ask if an epistemologically oriented philosopher is a good guide to literary interpretation.[10] We are also to ask what happens to the theory if the philosopher's interpretation of a work is shown inappropriate, misguided or simply bad. Nevertheless, cognitivists have, to a great extent, ignored real readers and the actual effects the works might have.

Catherine Wilson – who thinks that literary works may supply their readers non-propositional knowledge – argues that in learning in general, '[the] changes may lie, in one sense, behind the scenes: a person may be quite incapable of explaining how he perceives things now. But his learning must amount to some difference in what he is prepared to do or say under certain conditions'.[11] Assumedly, literary works may have both conscious and unconscious effects on their readers' attitudes and comprehension. But even though learning from literature would happen 'behind the scenes', the changes should manifest themselves somehow in a person's thoughts, attitudes, perception or behaviour. Of late, psychological studies have attempted to capture such changes.

The laboratory

In recent years, many philosophers have been eager to look at the sciences of the mind in order to advance the debate on literature and cognition. According to the naturalistic approach, promoted by philosophers such as Currie, philosophers should in the first place turn their eyes to psychological studies on actual readers. Because we, that is, human beings, have similar imaginative capacities and structure of the mind, together with certain shared cultural beliefs and attitudes, we are claimed to respond to fictional works basically the same way.[12] The study of these naturalistic tendencies is believed to shed light on philosophical issues.

At the same time, there has been a growing interest in the cognitive and emotive effects of literary narratives in psychology and neurosciences. The results of recent empirical psychological studies are diverse and controversial, and it is open to dispute what they can be said to show. Nevertheless, to mention some examples, studies have purported to show that readers gain both true and false information from fictional narratives;[13] that learning from literature happens as a result of imaginative engagement with the work, by readers' 'transporting' themselves into the storyworld;[14] and that fictional narratives have long-term impact on their readers' actual beliefs, their impact even increasing over time.[15] Further, the studies purport to show that fictional stories foster empathy and emotional perception and improve social cognition,[16] and that reading literature can lead to positive personality changes.[17] Moreover, the studies and reflection on them suggest that works of literature may deepen readers' self-understanding;[18] that fictions stimulate reflection on the ethical matters they explore;[19] that fictions might help readers in forming coherent autobiographical narratives;[20] that fictions help tolerate ambiguity;[21] and that literature helps in dehabituation or defamiliarization, so that through literary reading we are enabled to contemplate alternative models for being in the world.[22]

In a recent study that gained much transdisciplinary interest and stirred a lot of controversy, psychologists David Comer Kidd and Emanuele Castano measured the affective and cognitive effects of reading literature, or more precisely, how reading short literary texts – short stories and excerpts of complete works – affects subjects' performance on tests of affective and cognitive theory of mind. In five experiments, the subjects were randomly assigned 'literary fiction', popular fiction or non-fiction, or were given no reading at all. The impact of reading was measured in tests that employ greyscale photographs of actors' eye-regions (Reading the Mind in the Eyes test or RMET), photographs of faces of people (The Diagnostic Analysis of Nonverbal Accuracy or DANVA), and cartoon outlines of facially expressed emotions (the Yoni task) and in which the subjects were to infer the persons' (actors' or cartoon characters') thoughts and emotions from the minimal visual cues (and linguistic, in the Yoni task).[23] The study claimed that the reading of literary fiction (but not genre fiction or non-fiction) improves people's ability to infer other persons' beliefs and motives (cognitive ToM) and their feelings (affective ToM).

Problems in empirical studies

Kidd and Castano's study and various other psychological studies of reading seem to initially support the cognitivist position. Nevertheless, they should certainly not be taken at face value. While psychologists themselves are often cautious in their conclusions, philosophers have expressed exceptional naivety in accepting the findings as such. Indeed, as Kathleen Stock puts it, 'surprisingly, given philosophers' tendencies to cautious critical analysis, the use of [empirical] evidence is not always inspected as scrupulously as it could be'.[24] Not enough attention has been given to matters such as the following: Were the narratives presented for the subjects complete literary narratives or brief artificial narratives devised especially for experimental purposes?[25] How were the works chosen? Were the control texts similar in relevant aspects? How were the subjects chosen? Was the number of participants sufficient? How was the material introduced to the subjects? What sort of instructions were they given? What were the tests used and what is their status in the scientific community? What, precisely, in the material caused the effects – certain literary features, narrative form, imaginative engagement? What was the finding – causation or correlation? Could other factors explain the results? Could the assumed changes produced by reading be long-term? And finally: Do the changes manifest in real-life interaction? Some of these questions need to be discussed in detail.

First, what is the actual object of these studies? The studies do not always differentiate between *literariness*, *narrativity* and *fictionality*. Some research attributes persuasive effect to *narrative form* in general, some to *fictionality* and others to *literary features* or *literariness*. What qualities in the works produce the effects, and are these qualities distinct to or characteristic of literature or fiction or narratives?[26] In the empirical studies, fiction is often contrasted with 'non-fiction'. But what is meant by that broad term? Memoirs or works in the history of experience, for instance, might perhaps invite immersion, stimulate the readers' imagination, perhaps even improve their empathic skills. Kidd and Castano, for their part, contrasted fictions which 'depicted at least two characters' with non-fictions which 'primarily focused on a nonhuman subject'.[27] In other words, there were other differences between the two selections apart from their fictionality or status as literature.[28] Moreover, literary fictions were contrasted to popular fictions that were not systematically selected.[29]

Second, it might be difficult to attribute the alleged changes to 'literariness' if the researchers are unsure about the definition of literature.[30] Often, the researchers rely on canonized and acclaimed works of literature and/or consider literature in textual (syntactic or semantic) terms: the 'literary' use of language is seen to deviate from ordinary use of language because of its ambiguity, unusual words or word sequence and the like.[31] Behind the view lies the Russian formalist conception of literariness and the ideas of foregrounding and defamiliarization. Such a textualist view of literature is problematic, however: literary works may be laconic and plain as for their language, whereas one can find ambiguity and symbolic meanings from informative texts if one looks for them.

Third, 'literature' or even 'literary fiction' is not one but many. It might not be wise to make general claims about *narratives*, *literature* or *fiction* on the basis of the findings that some narratives, works of literature or fictions have some (perhaps short-term) impacts on their readers' dispositions. For instance, Keith Oatley and his colleagues chose as their material Tolstoy's 'The Lady with the Toy Dog' (1899) – a realist fiction which describes an adulterous affair between an unhappily married banker Dmitri and a young married woman Anna – and which is in line with Oatley's assumption that fictional narratives are simulation of everyday social life and principally explore problems in the social world.[32] The critics ask if experimental works from writers such as Beckett and Kafka, for instance, would support the researchers' conclusions; further, would Nabokov's *Lolita* or Burroughs's *Naked Lunch* work as cases in Frank Hakemulder's model of literature as a moral laboratory in which readers may try different roles?[33] Likewise, Bal and his colleagues, who look for the value of literature in the workplace, assume the possibility that some fictions might be harmful, as in they might produce negative 'persistent affective and behavioural outcomes':[34]

> For instance, the novel *Das Schloss* by Kafka, showing the negative effects of bureaucratic systems, may lead to decreased faith in mankind, possibly leading to disengagement and ambivalence. Fictional narrative experiences may also lead to negative emotional reactions, such as anger, sadness, fear, and depression. Hypothetically, reading sad stories or watching sad movies may cause people to become less happy, possibly negatively influencing their self-image, and eventually leading to less social behavior and interference with work demands. Finally, fictional narratives may also present role models for employees on the workplace by presenting characters in a story who behave in ways consistent with moral beliefs of a reader or who go against these moral beliefs, and therefore educate a reader in moral agency.[35]

In turn, Katrina Fong and her colleagues assume that 'each fiction genre is likely to provide a distinctive conceptual framework through which readers construct meaning about the social world', and they expect variability in how different genres influence readers' social orientation.[36] Interestingly, their study found out that 'Romance was the only fiction genre that predicted greater interpersonal sensitivity after controlling for other forms of print-exposure and various individual differences'.[37]

Fourth, the tests used in the studies are an interesting topic of their own. It has been remarked that the RMET (Baron-Cohen et al. 1997, revised 2001) makes use of sophisticated vocabulary, such as *apologetic, dispirited, despondent, preoccupied, aghast, affectionate, tentative, imploring, defiant, pensive* and *incredulous*.[38] Some suggest that the act of reading in a certain way could prime verbal processing or temporarily increased vocabulary, leading to higher RMET scores.[39] Moreover, it is important to remember that cognitive empathy or social cognition is amoral and may be used for various purposes, including sadism. (Actually, psychopathic individuals do not score differently on the test than non-psychopathic individuals.[40]) The relation between RMET scores and social cognition – not to mention the relation between RMET scores and prosocial action – in real life has been questioned.[41] Even though an effect would be statistically significant, it might not be noticeable in real life. Maria Panero and her colleagues claim that '[a]ny immediate effect of reading on theory-of-mind abilities is likely to be fragile and depend not only on the individual reader and text, but also the relationship between the two'.[42] In turn, Currie remarks that short-term improvements in empathic tendencies are far from 'the controlled, reflective and discriminating use of empathy'[43] and that while trivial events might lead to immediate minor helping behaviour, they presumably do not lead to shifts in a person's moral outlook or dispositions.[44]

Fifth, the way a text is read arguably matters. Black and Barnes remark that 'participants across experiments may read in different ways depending on the instructions they are given and that reading in a laboratory setting and reading for pleasure may vary more broadly'.[45] Likewise, Panero and her colleagues expect that responses are likely to vary between cases in which one is reading for pleasure and in which one is reading with the knowledge of having to perform a series of tests after reading.[46]

Sixth, empirical studies have been criticized in that they do not account for the readers' individual differences. The effects a text has on its readers might vary greatly between the readers, depending on their cognitive abilities, social backgrounds and personal histories.[47] It has also been suggested that factors such as gender might affect whose point of view in a narrative they will adopt and with whom they will empathize (with people supposedly adopting the viewpoint they are familiar with).[48]

Seventh, linguistic competence does not yet make literary competence. Reading literature is not a natural activity, a stimulus–response mechanism, whose effects could be measured as one can measure how a human eye reacts to light. Instead, literary works are cultural artefacts whose *interpretation* requires skills and knowledge, such as knowledge of literary conventions and history.[49] Conversely, empirical research often challenges such a 'conventionalist' view and even prefers 'innocent' subjects; David S. Miall, for one, gives his attention to 'ordinary readers, who generally have little or no interest in interpreting texts in the ways this is typically done in literature classrooms'.[50] Miall is after 'certain processes of reading that may occur in any period' and which 'themselves are constituted by the cognitive and affective equipment that we possess in common with our reading ancestors'.[51] Information gained by studying innocent subjects might not, however, shed much light on the practice of literature or literary values. As Monika Fludernik puts it, '[t]he results obtained [by empirical psychological research] are frequently open to criticism from a literary angle, since the informants generally have little experience of reading and do not find it easy to understand the texts'.[52]

Eighth, the researchers generally admit that they cannot infer causal direction between fiction reading and empathy. Raymond Mar and his colleagues ponder:

> It would be slightly surprising if individuals who are naturally empathic and skilled socially were to prefer a solitary pursuit such as reading over their unhindered and easy interactions with peers in the real-world. The schema of a bookworm present in North American culture (and other cultures, such as in Japan), describes a child withdrawing from his or her social world (often due to rejection) into a world of fantasy wrought by narratives. It seems unlikely that this conception would have absolutely no basis in reality.[53]

Currie provides various reasons to doubt the enthusiastic views on the effects of fiction on moral cognition and behaviour: Perhaps empathizing with fictional characters is different from empathizing with real people as the stimuli available in fictional cases (direct access to a character's thoughts and feelings) is much richer than the stimuli available in real life; or perhaps empathy and helping behaviour are only weakly connected, if at all; or perhaps empathizing with fictional characters merely primes readers for empathizing with real people; or perhaps empathizing with fictional characters is actually rare in reading fiction. Further, he suggests that empathizing with fictional characters might even have a significant but *negative* effect on helping behaviour. Perhaps empathizing with fictional characters eats into readers' empathy capital and gives them a sense of responding well, lessening their desire to empathize with real people; or perhaps empathizing with fictional characters weakens the psychological connection between empathy and helping behaviour, as responses to fiction lack the action part.[54]

Despite his scepticism towards current empirical research on literary response, Currie thinks that the road to evidence, if any, is via empirical sciences. He argues that while it may be true that the experiments so far conducted do not 'target the conditions philosophers consider most conducive to literary education', such as sensitive subjects and highly valued literary works, that may be known only by taking an interest in the empirical work.[55] Indeed, Currie argues that philosophers should maintain an awareness of the state of the evidence and frame their hypotheses in ways that suggest how the tests may be carried out. Furthermore, he proposes that philosophical theories of the epistemic value of literature – how we *might* learn from literature – are still needed in order to provide explanatory options for psychological work.[56]

One might wonder whether cooperation between experimental psychologists and literary scholars might be the best way to gather evidence that would be experimentally rigorous and yet sensitive to the reading of literature. In fact, during recent decades, many literary scholars have been eager to apply the tools of experimental psychology and cognitive science to the interpretation of literary narratives. In cognitive poetics, literary interpretation is studied using psychological concepts, such as *schema* and *script*. According to schema theory, the interpretation of human experience is an automatic process, an act of identification, in which the subject organizes experiential information using her existing cognitive frameworks or concepts (*schemas*), such as gender roles and the structure of actions performed in repeated situations (*scripts*), such as visiting a restaurant.[57]

Literary scholars have, however, debated whether the interpretation of literary works could be reduced to the reader's act of employing her existing schemas. For example, those who support the idea of 'unnatural narratives' have argued that many literary works, especially those of an innovative sort, 'defy, flaunt, mock, play, and experiment with some (or all) of these core assumptions about narrative'.[58] As the literary scholar

Jan Alber sees it, 'some literary texts not only rely on but aggressively challenge the mind's fundamental sense-making capabilities'.[59] As noted, he maintains that literary works often twist readers' 'natural', everyday schemas, perhaps thus creating new conceptions.[60]

There is a worry that in using cognitive psychological concepts, literary scholars and philosophers outsource the epistemology of literature to psychology and submit to a narrow, natural scientific notion of knowledge. Moreover, the empirical psychological study and the 'neocognitivist's' position seem incompatible, for the former cannot get to subjective experiences and the latter is after the advancement of subjective (self-)understanding. The acquisition of *knowledge* from literature or short-term improvements in social cognition might perhaps be (to some extent) scientifically studied, but the neocognitivist notion of understanding is closer to a hermeneutic phenomenological conception of knowledge, or knowledge of a person's comprehensive experience of the world. If we construe understanding from the point of view of the reader's phenomenological experience of the work, it is difficult to see how the cognitive benefits of literature could ever allow quantification and measuring. How could we test, for instance, how literature helps us to see the *significance* of things, or gives *meaning* to our experiences or helps us to make our life-world? How to study how one's understanding of a concept, such as grief, or one's network of beliefs has changed as a result of reading? Such things can be evaluated only from the perspective of the subject who gives the work a meaning. The enhanced understanding gained by reading fictional literature is akin to happiness, marital satisfaction or a mechanic's comprehension of carburettors, in that it can be conceived only from the inside.[61] Put together, the view of reading as a cultural activity and the idea that understanding may only be grasped from the inside suggest that evidence, if any, is to be found elsewhere. First, they invite a look at literary interpretation as performed by professional readers.

The practice of criticism

For the first generation analytic aestheticians, the aim of aesthetics was, as Arnold Isenberg defines it in the conclusion of his 1950 report to the Rockefeller Foundation, '*an analysis of the concepts and principles of criticism* and other aesthetic studies, such as the psychology of art'.[62] Since Monroe C. Beardsley's pioneering work, subtitled 'Problems in the Philosophy of Criticism', many analytic aestheticians have considered their field a second-order discipline – metacriticism – that aims at clarifying and refining critical terms and principles by investigating the practice of criticism. This is a view which Richard Shusterman, for instance, still emphasized in his introduction for the anthology *Analytic Aesthetics* (1989).[63]

Many, if not most, contemporary analytic aestheticians think, however, that the study of the fundamental issues in criticism – its methods, aims and concepts – is not only too narrow but also a misguided description of aesthetics.[64] Indeed, Beardsley's tripartite distinction, in which the *philosopher* studies what the *critic* says about the *poet's* work,[65] is no longer tenable (if it ever was). Lamarque, for one, has forcefully demonstrated that criticism is too diverse a field for a methodologically coherent view of it to be presented and that metacriticism will fail both as a descriptive and as a normative exercise: because of the multiplicity of critical approaches, *descriptive metacriticism*, which aims to explain critical principles, could only deliver a set of principles relative to each approach. In turn, *normative metacriticism*, which aims to formulate interpretative principles that ought to be followed, would simply describe the principles of a given approach, and the validity of those principles would become disputed after the critical approach had been declined.[66] Moreover, the philosophy of literature cannot be construed as metacriticism because of its concern for questions falling outside criticism. Nonetheless, there are some contemporary aestheticians who think that philosophy of literature consists to a large part of metacriticism. For example, in *On Criticism* (2009), Noël Carroll maintains 'that the time has come to rejuvenate [metacriticism], since there is probably more art criticism being produced and consumed now than ever before in the history of the world'.[67] Similarly, Stephanie Ross proposes that 'ideal critics inform us about aesthetic properties, propose interpretations, and offer summary evaluations'.[68] The idea of philosophy of literature as metacriticism is also implicit in many contemporary analytic philosophers' work.

Although they are critical of the metacritical approach for good reasons, Lamarque and Olsen think that if literary works had cognitive value as works of literature, we would expect to find evidence for it from the practice of criticism. Lamarque and Olsen themselves think that the lack of debate on literary *truths* in criticism implies that truth is not a literary value:[69] academic critics are not generally interested in knowledge-acquisition from fiction and matters alike. But here, too, the definition of *cognition* is extremely important. In the neocognitivist approach that builds on the concept of understanding, criticism looks like a true treasure chamber. Critical analyses of how a given work challenges the reader's conceptual thinking, questions her standard conceptions and provides her new categories, for instance, give valuable evidence – and insight – for the neocognitivist. Literary histories describe what sort of cognitive values literary works have been given in different periods and literary genres. The critic Rita Felski, for one, writes:

> As selfhood becomes self-reflexive, literature comes to assume a crucial role in exploring what it means to be a person. The novel, especially, embraces a heightened psychological awareness, meditating on the murky depths of motive and desire, seeking to map the elusive currents and by-ways of consciousness, highlighting countless connections and conflicts between self-determination and socialization. Depicting characters engaged in introspection and soul-searching, it encourages its readers to engage in similar acts of

> self-scrutiny. It speaks to a distinctively modern sense of individuality – what one critic calls improvisational subjectivity – yet this very conviction of personal uniqueness and interior depth is infused by the ideas of others. One learns how to be oneself by taking one's cue from others who are doing the same. From the tormented effusions of young Werther to the elegiac reflections of Mrs Dalloway, the novel spins out endless modulations on the theme of subjectivity.[70]

And the critic Jesse Matz, commenting on the modernist movement in literature:

> [T]he novel inherited by the moderns [. . .] seemed essentially traditional – slow, staid, set, and so unable to match the flux, the bewilderment, the excitement that now defined modern life. Therefore the moderns tried to 'make it new' by trading the novel's regular forms for experimental forms of flux, perplexity, openness, skepticism, freedom, and horror. They replaced omniscience with fixed or fallible perspectives, broke their chapters into fragments, made sex explicit, and dissolved their sentences into the streams and flows of interior psychic life.[71]

Of great importance are, of course, critical descriptions of particular literary works. The critic Robin Feuer Miller says that in *Brothers Karamazov*, Dostoyevsky asks us to contemplate 'great questions', such as the problem of evil and the overcoming of grief felt at the loss of a child.[72] For the critic Malcolm V. Jones, the novel 'echoes and develops some of the most ancient paradoxes and preoccupations of humanity' and is capable of 'plumbing and illuminating the depths of the human soul'.[73] In reading the work, we are invited to perform *moral* enquiries, for we 'find ourselves drawn from our focus on the murder story to questions of moral responsibility and guilt, complicity and collusion'.[74] Moreover, Jones thinks that this contemplating is not limited to the reading of the work, as 'its characters and the dramatic events in which they participate continue to agitate the memory long after the book has been put down'.[75]

Criticism illuminates how literary works treat philosophical, ethical, political and other themes. They describe in detail how literary works express and explore the abstract themes they are about, problematize their own interpretations and provide us unsophisticated readers various new ways to look at the works. On the face of it, the neocognitivist approach seems compatible with academic literary analysis; with certain literary genres and writers, 'cognitive matters' seem even essential. Yet, the question of *perlocution*, the actual effect works have on their real readers, remains. In critical analysis, the cognitive function of literature is commonly approached in terms of *implicit readers*. We are shown how the works can be read, or perhaps ought to be read. Following the critic's interpretive suggestions may lead to rewarding readings, perhaps cognitive 'payoff' too.

Further, academic and lay readers might differ both in their motives for reading and in what they believe they have gained from reading. (Which motives fall within the 'literary stance' is a matter of dispute however.) Noël Carroll, for one, has argued that ideas which academic philosophers find trivial in literature may be important for a nonacademic lay reader.[76] Carroll claims that philosophers have not paid enough attention to the common reader but 'often build their theories in response to certain epistemological constraints that have little to do with the actual reception of art'.[77] After pointing the way to 'the actual reception of art', Carroll, however, reverts to his armchair view of the general interests of 'typical consumers of art and literature'.[78] The question of actual reception needs to be explored. Ideally, we could have information on real readers in their 'natural habitat'.

The practice of literature

In debating the cognitive value of literature, cognitivists and anti-cognitivists tend to disagree about what the 'common reader' looks for in literature. Eileen John, for one, thinks that readers frequently take a philosophical, that is, conceptual analytical, attitude to certain kinds of literary works.[79] Lamarque objects to John's claim by saying that readers seldom have '"cognitive" expectations', for they 'are not commonly motivated to read such works by the thought that they will learn something'.[80] Lamarque states that the conceptual clarification which John describes rather 'looks like a contingent by-product of reading'.[81] Is it? The aprioristic debate quickly arrives at a dead end. Moreover, speculations about *typical literary responses* seem futile as there is information concerning common readers, the consumers of literature. The question is rather how to interpret these results (or perform more comprehensive future studies) and what to infer from them.

In addition to the practice of academic literary analysis that provides us information about how professional readers interpret literary works, there are studies of literary reception as conducted by general readers, other than those done in the psychology lab. Some of these studies are explicitly after the question of how texts change the minds and lives of actual readers.[82] Reception studies carried out within literary studies cover various matters from an individual works' reception history to literary sociological studies of the interests of contemporary audiences. Some studies employ interviews in studying *qualitatively* actual readers and their reasons for reading. What makes literary reception studies important for the cognitivist is that they examine the reading of complete literary works in the actual setting – the literary practice – and, further, that many of them are conducted by educated experts.

Literary historical studies on the reception of particular works illustrate how given artworks have been approached and understood in different times. Such studies are important in showing, for example, that for the readers of *Brothers Karamazov*, 'cognitive expectations' have always been central.[83] On the other hand, reception-historical study on newspaper criticism, for instance, sheds light on the sort of (ideologically coloured) guidance and reading models offered to layreaders.

Further, literary sociological studies on actual readers give rough views of the interests of the general reading public and shed light on the sort of values they look for in literature. Interestingly, such studies suggest that while people report reading fictional literature primarily for pleasure, that is, entertainment and relaxation, their motive to gain knowledge or enlightenment from reading or to reflect on humanly interesting themes via literature, is also significant. In leisure reading, central motives include obtaining intellectual enrichment and a broader view of life; typical motives include structuring one's life and providing oneself with an identity.[84] These studies suggest that 'cognitive expectations' are common among the readers.

While literary sociological studies may ideally tell us important things about real readers and reading cultures, it is easy to find weak spots also in studies of the kind. For example, the sociological approach to readers' motives is problematic when it makes use of *surveys*. Are the questions asked in the survey relevant to readers outside the survey? Can we suppose that the participants had a clear view about their motives before the survey? Can we expect that they already had a view of the value or significance of literature? In surveys, people tend to appear competent and morally good, especially when they do not master the issue at hand; they tend to give socially desirable answers.[85] 'Has some literary work changed your life permanently? Have you learnt profound insights in literature? Has reading improved your self-understanding and increased your acuity?' Such questions would beg affirmative answers.[86] Moreover, the questions asked, or the answer options provided, may simply be too vague and shed very little light on the sort of 'knowledge' people look for in literature, for instance; oftentimes, the studies do not differentiate between the important concepts *fiction* and *literature*.

In order to access readers' subjective experiences we have to consult the readers themselves. When we move from questionnaires and quantitative study to personal interviews and qualitative study, we can approach (but not access) readers' personal experiences. Unlike in questionnaires, in personal interviews the interviewer may probe or ask follow-up questions, clarification, elaboration. Instead of yes/no answers to the question whether readers *feel* that they have improved their self-understanding by reading, we might want them to describe the insights they believe they have gained from reading particular works.

In examining the advancement of understanding, the philosopher Linda Zagzebski argues that when Plato speaks of episteme, it connects with *techne* – practical human arts or skills, from cooking to medicine to shipbuilding. Understanding is a *skill* and it manifests itself in *use*. For Zagzebski, the test for success in understanding is largely within the practice, *techne* itself. She maintains that '[r]eliably carrying out the goals of a *techne* can be verified within the *techne*. One's understanding of an art work can be proven by successfully giving that understanding to others by teaching it in an art history class.'[87] Making one's understanding public makes it an object of learning and a subject of assessment and development.

Besides the two promising sources of evidence, or aspects to it, critical analysis and literary reception studies, evidence for the cognitivist might be found within the practice of literature: from readers' self-imposed descriptions of their literary experiences, especially as expressed in non-fictional writings that traditionally link to the arts and emphasize one's influences and attitudes to life – essay and autobiography.[88] The learning scientist Lorraine Foreman-Peck noticed some decades ago that 'it appears that most people are unaware of what they have learnt from reading literature, unless what they have learnt has been very remarkable and with far-reaching consequences'.[89] Cognitivists have typically looked for transformative reading experiences and cited well-known anecdotes of particular thinkers' situations and the impact literature had on them. A common example is that of John Stuart Mill who overcame his depression in the wake of reading Wordsworth and learnt that 'there was real, permanent happiness in tranquil contemplation'.[90] Other frequently cited cases are those of Freud, who supposedly found his psychological theories anticipated in Sophocles and Shakespeare, and Wittgenstein, who recommended Tolstoy's *Hadshi Murat* to Norman Malcolm, who had characterized war as 'a boredom',[91] with the intention of opening his friend's eyes to the real nature of war.

Here is another example. In his memoirs, the philosopher Georg Henrik von Wright describes one of his intellectual awakenings:

> In my solitary walks in Buenos Aires [in 1968] my mind was occupied by disturbances in Paris and other parts of the world. I came to a deep realization about Dostoyevsky's story about the Grand Inquisitor. I felt as if I understood the profound, tragic meaning of life and history: if a man should carry out his natural ability to do good, he would have to have a freedom to do evil. One requires the other. The powers of self-preservation and self-annihilation keep each other in balance in man. I mention this episode, because it gave me the attitude that still determines my thinking. It is not objective knowledge, but a way, though not the only way, to contemplate life.[92]

Von Wright's statement is very impressive: a literature-inspired episode during which he deeply understood the tragic meaning of life and which gave him an attitude that came to determine his thinking and writing. Yet, testimonies, when used as evidence, should be taken with reservations. If questionnaires are vulnerable to social desirability, the same goes for testimonies represented in literary form, such as in essays and autobiographies. In public exclamations, the writer is liable to many sorts of literary influences and conventions on how to write about literature. The idea of transformative reading experiences is a commonplace in the humanist tradition, and the romantic idea of art-based epiphany might aestheticize and guide the author's understanding and telling of her experience. Epiphanies, profound realizations and other emotionally strong epistemic revelations might be best reflected upon with care.[93] In his essay 'Against Epiphanies', the author Charles Baxter notes that 'in retrospect, I can say with some certainty that most of my own large-scale insights have turned out to be completely false. They have arrived with a powerful, soul-altering force; and they have all been dead wrong.'[94] Indeed, we should be suspicious of such feelings, for they may stem from a coherent set of misbeliefs, for example. The invention of phlogiston must have produced a eureka-feeling: suddenly everything makes sense. In literature, in turn, an author can 'manipulate the parameters', so to say, and produce an illusion of understanding – an affective truth, something that *rings true*, perhaps, – and we are led to think that this is, say, what *life* is about. Just because the depiction is coherent and vivid (and emotional!).

Furthermore, the problems of self-assessment are still around. According to research in the sciences of the mind, we ought to suspect our metacognitive skills, including our assessment of what we have learnt and from where. As Petri Ylikoski concludes from psychological studies, 'most people are prone to feel that they understand the world with far greater detail, coherence, and depth than they really do.'[95] Currie, in turn, remarks that self-understanding is unreliable and governed by irrational principles.[96] As he puts it, '[e]verything we know about our understanding of ourselves suggests that we are not very good at knowing how we got to be the kind of people we are. In fact we don't really know, very often, what sorts of people we are.'[97] Nevertheless, the fact that there are problems in self-reflection – that we have cognitive biases or that we crumble in self-understanding – does not make self-reflection useless. Rather, we ought to learn about those biases and how they affect our thinking. Our knowledge of cognitive biases helps us to suspect and refine our judgement, and after we acknowledge and understand our tendencies to err, we might perhaps learn to avoid their excesses.[98]

Of course, our knowledge of readers' actual responses to literary works does not solve any philosophical debates. Moreover, studies of literary reception are more or less contingent, as they deal with particular literary cultures, particular works and particular readers. Of course, literary reception studies require interpretation and critical consideration as for their aims, concepts, methods and results. Interviews and testimonies are problematic sources of evidence. Nevertheless, looking at descriptions of personal literary experiences and literary reception studies can shed light on the *values* which people look for in literature and hopefully give an insight into what people think they have *gained* from reading the works. Do they look for 'insight, revelation, and enlarged comprehension' in reading literature and do they report to see things in a new light after reading works? At least von Wright did; in his later life, he wrote several philosophical essays on the insights he had drawn from Dostoyevsky and other authors.

I agree with those who are sceptical of the cognitive value of literature in that the cognitivist has to support her claims about the cognitive value of literature with evidence stronger than a mere reference to the textual features of the works. At the same time, I am afraid that there is no direct way to such evidence. As for its methodology, the philosophy of literature is perhaps best considered in a pluralistic fashion. It needs (i) a *metacritical element* in order to understand what it is to approach a literary work as an artwork, and if the enhancement of understanding is an important literary phenomenon, one will find evidence for it from the practice of criticism. Nevertheless, academic literary analysis is theory-driven and does not represent all the values that general readers search for in literature; nor does *critical analysis* examine the perlocutionary effects of the works. It is thus important for a philosophical survey to also have (ii) a constraint from the *actual practice* of literature. While the reception of literature can be studied from various viewpoints, I propose that a philosopher would benefit most from looking at literary historical and sociological reception studies conducted by literary scholars, for such studies are acquainted with theories of reading and examine the actual practice of literature. Finally, in understanding *how* literary works *actually* advance one's understanding and affect one's thought, we need (iii) the subject's, the reader's, point of view, to which documents such as essays and autobiographies provide one route.

What is the role of the philosophy of literature, then? It is in the overall analysis of the phenomenon of literature. As for studying the cognitive benefits of literature, there are philosophical issues, such as the notion of 'cognitive value' and the relation between aesthetic and cognitive values in literature. Moreover, critics' descriptions of literary works' cognitive content are often metaphorical, especially when the works provide new viewpoints or violate commonplaces, and expressions such as the 'plumbing and illuminating the depths of the human soul' call for epistemological scrutiny.

Even if the results of empirical studies of literary reception were univocal and proved that reading fictional literature has so-called cognitive benefits, the fact that people learn from literature is not much of a discovery. After all, various sorts of things may 'enhance our understanding', and yet we hesitate to call these things, such as gossiping about one's neighbour, cognitive practices.[99] A philosophical theory would need to account for the distinctive features of literary cognition, that is, how literary works provide heightened perception in a unique way, as works of literature. This essay has attempted to do so with reference to the literary narrative form and the mode of imaginative engagement literary works invite in the reader.

Objectivist and relational cognitivism

Many philosophers and literary theorists alike have been suspicious of references to actual readers because of the assumed idiosyncrasy or contingency of the response. The literary critic Jonathan Culler, for example, warned one of the 'the dangers of an experimental or socio-psychological approach which would take too seriously the actual and doubtless idiosyncratic performance of individual readers'.[100] Many early reception theorists were also sceptical of the study of real individual readers. Wolfgang Iser, for one, thought that such studies could lead to 'uncontrolled subjectivism', and that a theory of aesthetic response could be accused of sacrificing 'the text to the subjective arbitrariness of comprehension'.[101] Likewise, in analytic philosophy of literature, which has its roots in text-oriented literary critical approaches such as formalism and New Criticism, the turn towards the reader and her role in constructing the meaning of the work is suspect because of its assumedly subjectivistic outcome.

When studying literary interpretation, analytic philosophers have emphasized the notions of *meaning* and *intention* in literature, an interest which stems from the philosophy of language. In the philosophy of literature, a common line of thought maintains that a literary work (ideally) has a determinate meaning that is achieved by some sort of act of recovery: by looking for the intentions of the author, the beliefs and expectations of the author's 'ideal' audience or the textual meaning of the work supplemented with knowledge about the work's context of origin. Further, the work meaning is typically considered autonomous or fixed, and admissions of the reader's active role in constructing the meaning of the work in interpretation are easily seen to lead to unwelcome relativism.

In analytic philosophy of literature, the cognitivist is required to show that learning from literature is integral to literary interpretation. Her task is to demonstrate what we can learn from the work and, further, 'that what we claim to have learnt from an artwork is a point, insight, or truth, *that is to be found in the artwork itself*, as John Gibson characterizes the cognitivist position.[102] One can doubt to what extent there are objective insights in literature that reside in the works themselves and exist independently of an interpretative framework.[103]

A distinction between 'objectivist' and 'relational' cognitivism, or 'meaning' and 'significance', is perhaps in place here. Often, we are interested in the assumed authorial meaning of a work. But if we limit ourselves to the recovery of meaning, we miss a lot both intellectually and aesthetically. In his exhaustive work on literary imagination, the critic Bo Pettersson proposes detailed analyses of ways by which literary works may impart knowledge. Nevertheless, he adds:

> But that knowledge and how to use or benefit from it can lead to a range of responses: you can learn about different ways of life, by emulating or rejecting them; understand the workings of unreliability better; entertain the thought of hypothetical action; solve a riddle or meet a challenge in your imagination. And all such forms of benefit can of course be slanted or inverted in the course of reading. So what the audience learns is never clear, not least owing to the fact that people interpret literature in such different ways. [. . .] For instance, readers of a didactic poem may be put off by its patronizing tone and perhaps 'learn' the opposite of what was intended. They benefit in some sense, but this is not necessarily what the poet, according to Horace, intended.[104]

Some philosophers that have been labelled 'anticognitivists' in this essay believe that literary works may have significant cognitive value, but they state that this value is reader-relative and not integral to the works as literary works. They argue that the cognitive value of art is contingent and dependent on individual ways of reading. Richard Posner, for one, thinks that

> Instead [of providing practical tips about life] literature helps us, as Nietzsche would have put it, to become what we are. The characters and situations that interest us in literature are for the most part characters and situations that capture aspects of ourselves and our situation. Literature helps us make sense of our lives, helps us to fashion an identity for ourselves. If you don't already sense that love is the most important thing in the world, you're not likely to

be persuaded that it is by reading Donne's love poems, or Stendhal, or Galsworthy. But reading them may make you realize that this *is* what you think, and so may serve to clarify yourself to yourself.[105]

Lamarque, in turn, proposes that attending to literary works 'can shape the mind by inducing and guiding thoughts and thought processes' and that literary works 'can reconfigure our minds, usually, although not inevitably, in positive ways.'[106] However, he continues:

> What we go on to do with the thoughts thus accumulated is another matter altogether. They might affect our subsequent actions and attitudes, they might re-order our conception of ourselves. They might have no practical effect whatsoever. But any effects they do have will be contingent and largely dependent on local psychological dispositions of individual readers. It would be wrong to read back into the novels themselves – as somehow part of the very content of the novels – any such variable, reader-relative, and instrumental cognitive gains.[107]

Is it, then, that one may learn from a given work of art just anything? Rather than relativistic, I propose literary cognition to be understood as relational. Understanding is a skill, and unlike knowledge, it is a *property of a person*. David Cooper remarks that 'It is we who connect, relate, structure, order, assimilate, differentiate, exemplify, summarize, detail, and emphasize. All these actions involve choices on our part, choices for which we find good reasons in our experience of the physical world and of our fellow human beings.'[108] We can speak of the *breadth* and *depth* of understanding: understanding can be about different aspects of a phenomenon and those aspects may be understood in various degrees (and, of course, different ways). Consider a professor of Swedish history. This imaginary professor – who resembles Jens Ljundggren from Stockholm University – has a *broad* understanding of the reasons why compulsory gymnastics was introduced in Swedish schools in 1880, its scientific background and all its ideological, functional and social impact. The professor is able to embed his coherent body of true beliefs about the matter into a more comprehensive understanding of Swedish history – he sees how school gymnastics and conscription were part of the same project – and, further, he sees the ideals of Renaissance humanism that underlie school gymnastics. He may also have a *deep* understanding. He has an enormous amount of beliefs about school gymnastics in the end of the nineteenth century, and there are a lot of causal relations between these beliefs. For this reason, the professor and his student assess new studies, or claims, about the history of school gymnastics differently. The professor might consider a new claim highly significant, while the student considers it just another fact about the matter. They give the truths different significance, or different explanatory value, and different places in their system of beliefs.

The cognitive effects of a work of literature partly depend on the reader's literary competence and the interpretive frame they use, partly on the reader's background knowledge on which the fiction operates and partly on the reader's interests at the time. For this reason, we might not understand what we thought we found in a formative fiction of our youth, be it *Steppenwolf* or *The Stranger* or something similar. It is not that we now construe the insight differently, or consider it naive, but we cannot even bring the insight into our mind. We cannot find it in the book, for the insight was produced in a relation with the content and a background that has radically changed since – our beliefs and attitudes. Of course, the work matters. Some complicated or puzzling, perhaps even confusing works stay interesting. Elgin suggests that because Madame Bovary 'admits of multiple, increasingly sophisticated interpretations, [it] continues to enlighten. As our understanding evolves, we develop the capacity to glean new insights from it.'[109] At different times, different aspects come to the fore. No reading deflates the book.

Afterword

In addition to reassessing the notion of cognitive value, we ought to re-examine the demand for the cognitive value of literature which is clearly too strict. Anticognitivists often imply that in order to be cognitively valuable, artistic insights ought to be highly significant; perhaps even equal to that of scientific discoveries.[110] Obviously, this is partly due to cognitivists' grandiose claims of the beneficial effects of literature and their eagerness to place art on a par with science, together with the high emotional impact many works of art have on us.[111] Transformative reading experiences are offered as a paradigm for learning from literature and an analogue to (a rather naive view of) scientific progress and transformative experiences in philosophical theorizing.

The study of learning suggests that the knowledge we gather from (text)books does not stay long with us. The reading of non-fiction, such as essays, biographies and journals, might only seldom offer readers revolutionary changes in their world view or insights that stay with them for the rest of their lives. More often, learning from non-fiction *assumedly* amounts to slight changes in the reader's understanding of things. *Perhaps* even the readers of self-help guides soon forget the informative content of the works – not to mention acting upon that information – although the guides are written and read in order to (completely) change one's life. *Presumably*, a large part of the 'cognitive content' of both non-fiction and fiction is in the works inspiring one on one's journey. Albeit this is a philosophical conversation, a little amount of practical realism might be in place here. Many of us read different sorts of texts all the time, and we soon forget the source of a thought, point or argument we have encountered somewhere. Further, supposedly many of our ideas are combinations of points we have gathered from various sources, our present interest guiding our attention. Literary works might bring ideas to our attention and perhaps encourage us to find reasons for believing and adopting them.[112]

Again, many might object that the neocognitivist notion of understanding, at least the 'relational' rendering offered here, makes the cognitive outcome of literature too contingent. *What* is it that we learn in literature? Does a given work enhance our understanding in a certain way, say, under the perspective of authorial control, or is it that literature *influences* more than *educates* us? Von Wright, for instance, speaks of his impression and suggests that the insight he has gained from *Brothers Karamazov* has a subjective and affective dimension.

But does this lead to a position we have to avoid? Do we want to stick to the rather questionable idea of 'objective meaning' of a literary work and maintain that the cognitive content of a literary work is fixed and will be automatically grasped in the act of reading? Indeed, the turn from knowledge to understanding implies a difficult move from text to experience, marked by complex imagining, engagement with narrative and shifts of perspective and purpose. Clearly, a great deal of theoretical work is needed to properly establish such moves, but the road seems worth taking.

Notes

Chapter 1

1. The effects of reading literature, including its cognitive impact, have been studied in psychology for decades. For pioneering studies, see, for example, the works of Willie van Peer, Donald Kuiken, David S. Miall, Richard J. Gerrig and Deborah Prentice. For a historical overview of such empirical psychological studies, see Hakemulder 2000.
2. Brinkmann 2017.
3. Hakemulder, Fialho and Bal 2016, p. 31.
4. Bal and Veltkamp 2013, p. 2; Bal, Butterman and Bakker 2011.
5. Bal, Butterman and Bakker 2011, pp. 365–6.
6. Paul 2013.
7. Postmedia News, *National Post* 19 June 2013, https://nationalpost.com/entertainment/books/reading-literary-fiction-can-lead-to-an-better-decision-making-study-finds
8. Belluck 2013.
9. Chiaet 2013.
10. Greenfieldboyce 2013.
11. Lukits 2016.
12. Schonfeld 2013.
13. Haden 2015.
14. Almendrala 2016.
15. Whiteman 2016.
16. Beres 2017.
17. Trombetta 2017.
18. Josh Jones, *Open Culture* 11 January 2018, http://www.openculture.com/2018/01/how-reading-increases-your-emotional-intelligence-brain-function.html

19 Bergland 2014.
20 Bergado 2014.
21 In recent decades, the value of reading and studying literature has been defended in a variety of works, such as Harold Bloom's *How to Read and Why* (2000), Glenn C. Arbery's *Why Literature Matters: Permanence and the Politics of Reputation* (ISI Books, 2001), J. Hillis Miller's *On Literature* (2002), Frank B. Farrell's *Why Does Literature Matter?* (Cornell, 2004), Mark William Roche's *Why Literature Matters in the 21st Century* (Yale University Press, 2004), Rita Felski's *Uses of Literature* (Wiley-Blackwell, 2008), Daniel R. Schwarz's *In Defense of Reading: Teaching Literature in the Twenty-First Century* (2008), Martha C. Nussbaum's *Not for Profit: Why Democracy Needs the Humanities* (Princeton University Press, 2010), *Why Study Literature?* Edited by Jan Alber et al. (Aarhus University Press, 2011), Alan Jacobs's *The Pleasures of Reading in an Age of Distraction* (Oxford University Press, 2011), Andy Mousley's *Literature and the Human: Criticism, Theory, Practice* (CRC Press, 2013), Robert P. Waxler's *The Risk of Reading: How Literature Helps Us to Understand Ourselves and the World* (Bloomsbury, 2014), *Values of Literature*, edited by Hanna Meretoja et al. (Brill, 2015), Andrew Bennett and Nicholas Royle's *This Thing Called Literature: Reading, Thinking, Writing* (Routledge, 2015), Karen Swallow Prior's *On Reading Well: Finding the Good Life through Great Books* (Baker Publishing, 2018), and Robert Eaglestone's *Literature: Why It Matters* (Polity, 2019). The value of the study of the humanities has been argued for in books such as Geoffrey Galt Harpham's *The Humanities and the Dream of America* (University of Chicago Press, 2011), *The Public Value of the Humanities*, edited by Jonathan Bate (Bloomsbury, 2011), Stefan Collini's *What Are Universities for?* (Penguin, 2012), Helen Small's *The Value of the Humanities* (Oxford University Press, 2013), Michael Bérubé and Jennifer Ruth's, *The Humanities, Higher Education, and Academic Freedom: Three Necessary Arguments* (Palgrave Macmillan, 2015), for instance.
22 See, for example, Zunshine 2006.

23 See Felski 2008, p. 26.
24 See Zamir 2007, pp. 44–5.
25 Gibson 2007, p. 2.
26 Gibson 2007, p. 2; emphasis in original.
27 Goldman 2013, p. 12.
28 Goldman 2013, p. 8.
29 Gaskin 2013, p. 64.
30 Harrison 2015, p. 1.
31 Harrison 2015, p. 2.
32 Harrison 2015, p. 11.
33 Zamir 2019.
34 See Mikkonen 2013, pp. 9–12.
35 Cave 2014, p. 2; emphasis added.
36 After writing this, I came across baby porridge which its manufacturer advertises as 'contributing to normal cognitive development and understanding in children' because of the high level of iron in it. The claim is based on a clinical nutrition study partly financed by the company.
37 In psychology, the cognitive value of literature, its impact on social cognition, for instance, is often associated with immersion – the reader 'transporting' herself into the story. Psychological studies attempt to capture the changes which literary works might have on their readers but of which the readers might not themselves be aware.
38 Gros 2015.
39 See Lamarque 2010a, pp. 210–11.
40 See, for example, Cave (2016, p. 141) for a list of cognitive functions of storytelling.
41 Yet, dogmatism ought to be avoided here, and as Rita Felski (2008, p. 84) remarks, 'we should be wary of yoking genres too tightly to a particular epistemology by presuming, for instance, that realism strives to master and map the world, whereas modernism testifies to an unalloyed crisis of knowledge and representation.'
42 Booth 1988, p. 56. See also Landy's (2012, pp. 6–8) remarks on the suitability of different fictions for different cognitive purposes.

Chapter 2

1. For an excellent overview of different conceptions of imagination, see Fabian Dorsch's *Unity of Imagining* (2012).
2. See Austin (1975/1962) and Searle (1975). Searle speaks of two sorts of pretence: pretending *that* (third-person narratives) and pretending *to be* (first-person narratives).
3. Wolterstorff 1980, p. 233; emphasis in original.
4. See, for example, Matravers 2001, pp. 39–40.
5. For a view of different kinds of imagining (*de re*, *de se*, *de dicto*) in the report model, see Alward (2006).
6. Walton 1990, pp. 37–9.
7. See Currie 1990, pp. 22, 24–6 and 30–1; for another author-centric view, see Novitz 1987, p. 360.
8. Schopenhauer 1974, p. 554.
9. Schopenhauer 1974, p. 554.
10. Poulet 1969, pp. 55 and 58.
11. Poulet 1969, p. 57. Another's mind or a second self? Is there a unified subject behind a text? Is not an author also a medium who communicates thoughts that come from *somewhere*?
12. Iser 1978, p. 291; see also Iser 1972, pp. 297–9 and 1987, p. 163.
13. Schopenhauer 1966, p. 3.
14. In addition to there being *fictions* within non-fictions, certain non-fictional works, such as Plato's dialogues or Schopenhauer's philosophical treatises, have *literary* merit and can be read focusing on their literary properties.
15. Englund 2011, p. 8.
16. Currie 1990, p. 21.
17. Currie 1990, p. 21.
18. Currie 2014a, p. 361; for the distinction between propositional and perceptual imagination, see Van Leeuwen 2011. Assumedly fictions employ literary devices that invite certain modes of imaging, such as visual imagining, *de se* imagining and emotional engagement, in a way that distinguishes literary imagining from more basic forms

of imagining. The characteristically literary devices and styles are commonly used in non-fictional writing (except, perhaps, the depiction of alien consciousness). References to the truth and truthfulness are an important topic of their own; for instance, advertising a tragic story as true, or 'based on actual events', is a classic attempt to strengthen its emotional intensity (and moral seriousness, perhaps).

19 For differences in theories of fictionality in English-speaking and German-speaking world, notably, their foci and extension, see Hempfer (2004).

20 Camp 2009, p. 107; emphasis in original.

21 Richard Kearney perceptively distinguishes three historical paradigms of (literary) imagination, each relating 'to a general disposition of understanding which governs a specific period and informs the specific way people conceptualize the relationship between imagination and reality'. The paradigms are the '*mimetic* paradigm of the premodern (i.e. biblical, classical and medieval) imagination; the *productive* paradigm of the modern imagination; and the *parodic* paradigm of the postmodern imagination'. Kearney illustrates the paradigms with metaphors: 'the "mimetic" privileges the referential figure of the *mirror*; the "productive" the expressive figure of the *lamp*; and the "parodic" the reflexive figure of a *labyrinth of looking-glasses*.' (Kearney 1988, p. 17; emphases in original.)

22 Camp 2009, p. 116.
23 Ingarden 1979, p. 50.
24 Ingarden 1979, p. 386.
25 See Ingarden 1979, p. 53.
26 Ingarden 1979, p. 52.
27 Ingarden 1979, p. 368.
28 Ingarden 1979, p. 369.
29 Iser 1978, p. 283.
30 Iser 1971, p. 2.
31 Iser 1978, p. 280.
32 Iser actually claims that 'the more a text tries to be precise [. . .], the greater will be the number of gaps between the views' (Iser 1971, p. 11).

33 See Iser 1978, p. 280. Iser maintains that 'a second reading of a piece of literature often produces a different impression from the first. The reasons for this may lie in the reader's own change of circumstances, still, the text must be such as to allow this variation. On a second reading familiar occurrences now tend to appear in a new light and seem to be at times corrected, at times enriched.' Ingarden (1979, p. 375), in turn, remarks that in different historical situations readers fill in gaps (places of indeterminacy) in different ways and look for different aesthetically relevant qualities in the work.

34 Eco 1994, p. 6.

35 Richardson 1825, p. 589; emphases in original.

36 Pillow 2009, p. 364.

37 Coleridge 1983, p. 304.

38 Coleridge 1983, p. 304. For the uses of the terms *imagination* and *fancy* in eighteenth-century English criticism, see Bullitt and Bate (1945) and Donald F. Bond's footnote to Addison's *Spectator* No. 11 (in Addison 1965, p. 536n).

39 Walton 1990, p. 60.

40 Walton 1990, p. 60.

41 See Walton 1990, p. 50. When exploring dreams and daydreams, Walton (1990, p. 43) suggests that there may be 'collaborative daydreams', for example, when scientists *decide* to collaboratively imagine travelling to Saturn in a rocket. In such a case, the scientists set themselves a rule prescribing certain imaginings. Nonetheless, Walton thinks that 'whatever is in fact imagined as part of the dream or daydream is to be imagined' (Walton 1990, p. 44) and that daydreamers may be attentive to their acts of imagining and 'their manner of generating fictional truths' (Walton 1990, p. 50).

42 Lamarque and Olsen 1994, p. 154.

43 Lamarque and Olsen 1994, p. 155; emphasis in original.

44 Lamarque 2009, pp. 243–4.

45 Lamarque 2009, pp. 243–4.

46 In 'external' reflections on the content of the work, in which the reader thinks about the content of the work in the light of reality, one moves

away from the work, too, although not towards imaginary worlds but reality.
47 Lamarque and Olsen 1994, p. 129.
48 Walton 1978, p. 21.
49 Walton 1990, pp. 49–50.
50 Walton 1978, p. 21.
51 Lamarque and Olsen make various nuanced distinctions and employ concepts that ought to be kept separate. In addition to the distinction between the fictive stance and the literary stance, they distinguish between 'internal' and 'external' perspectives to the content of a fiction. 'Internal perspective' relates to immersion, imaginative engagement with the work, whereas 'external perspective' is about considering the content of the work with regard to reality (e.g. reference and truth).
52 Lamarque and Olsen 1994, pp. 256 and 408–9.
53 Lamarque 2014, p. 166.
54 Here, see Roland Barthes's (2002, pp. 3–6) distinction between 'readerly' and 'writerly' texts (*texte lisible* and *texte scriptible*).
55 Here, see Lamarque 2014, p. 20.
56 Lamarque and Stein Olsen (1994, p. 250) argue that there are 'different constraints on imaginings' which govern, for instance, what counts as success or failure. They maintain that imagining involves different *ends* and different *consequences* in different practices. Whereas so-called knowledge-seeking uses of imagination are 'tested and judged against experience in terms of conformity to observed fact', there are no such pressures on the idle daydream at the other end.
57 Friend 2008, 2011, 2012; Matravers 2014.
58 The genre of the work of course affects our expectations, and 'development' and 'closure', narrowly understood, refer to realist literature. However, 'closure' may also be, as Carroll (2007b) has shown, a 'sense' or 'the phenomenological feeling of finality' that takes place when all the important questions posed by the narrative are answered. On the other hand, the representation of non-linear or fragmented experience, from layered or multiple viewpoints, also sets literary fictions apart from, say, journalistic narratives.

59 Our interest in the determinate truth in fiction varies from one genre to another.
60 Lamarque and Olsen 1994, ch. 10; see also Lamarque's principles of literary interpretation in Lamarque 2014, ch. 4.
61 Burke 2009.
62 Martin 2009.
63 Internet: https://www.penguinrandomhouse.com/books/312497/the-plantagenets-by-dan-jones/
64 See Matravers 2018.
65 Eco, a proponent of the idea of the 'model reader', does not, however, favour relativism (see, for example, Eco 1989, p. 3, 2002, pp. 23–4).
66 Eco 2002, p. 65.
67 Eco 1990, p. 57; see also Eco 1984, p. 9.
68 Eco 2002, pp. 68–9.
69 Eco 1990, p. 62.
70 By imaginative engagement, I mean a variety of responses which take place not only when one is reading the work or following the story but also after the work is finished, and which all include reflecting on, or thinking of, the story content, or entertaining its sense as (literally) unasserted. I thus use the term in a broader sense than pretence-like imagination which admittedly is a substantial, although partly genre-relative, form of imaginative engagement with fiction.
71 See Walton (1990, pp. 159–60). Walton, however, argues that in this case, an extrapolation based on the Reality Principle, in which the character is seen to suffer from an inherited neurological disorder, makes the reader's imaginative engagement with the work smoother and more vivid than an extrapolation based on the Mutual Belief Principle, in which the character is seen to be possessed by the devil. Following the Mutual Belief Principle, the imaginer in Walton's example has to leave out her actual religious convictions and scientific beliefs, for instance, whereas following the Reality Principle, the imaginer can 'transpose more of what is true (and what she knows to be true) about herself into the world of her game' (1990, p. 160).

72 Gibson 2004, p. 110.
73 Elgin 2000, pp. 223–4.
74 Noël Carroll (2007a, pp. 32 and 36–7), for one, has argued that approaching a realist novel in terms of the social and psychological insight the work is meant to deliver is part of the literary response to the work.
75 See, for example, Walton (1990, pp. 71, 78, 94) and Currie (1990, pp. 48–9).
76 Walton (1990, pp. 49–50) discusses these two perspectives mainly in terms of *participation* and *observation*, that is, attending to fictional propositions and noting the ways by which their fictionality is generated. Nonetheless, he (1990, p. 289) suggests that one's observing of one's own participation in a game of make-believe may have cognitive value as it 'may make it easier to see connections between possible or actual fictional experiences and actual or possible real-life ones'.
77 Lamarque and Olsen 1994, pp. 143–4.
78 Lamarque and Olsen 1994, p. 147. As Jerrold Levinson (1997, p. 967), in turn, perceptively remarks, '[e]valuations of works as naive, puerile, or shallow, or as penetrating, insightful, or wise, implicate assessments of the cognitive adequacy of those works in a way that is hard to get around.'
79 Lamarque and Olsen 1994, p. 148.
80 Lamarque and Olsen 1994, p. 148.
81 Lamarque and Olsen 1994, p. 148.
82 Lamarque and Olsen 1994, p. 148.
83 Lamarque and Olsen 1994, p. 148, pp. 147–8.
84 These effects have been acknowledged and studied in make-believe theories. Walton, for one, has approached them with his distinction between *participation* and *observation* and his notion of *reflexive representation*.
85 Kivy 2011, p. 81; emphasis in original; see also Kivy 2006, p. 109.
86 Kivy 2011, p. 84. See also A. Pettersson (2012, p. 54) for external considerations during pauses in reading.

Chapter 3

1. I will use the terms 'narrative' and 'story' interchangeably. Also, I will use synonymously the terms 'self', 'person' and 'personal identity'.
2. The literary scholar Barbara Hardy proclaimed in the 1970s that 'inner and outer storytelling [. . .] plays a major role in our sleeping and waking lives'. Hardy states that 'we dream in narrative, daydream in narrative, remember, anticipate, hope, despair, believe, doubt, plan, revise, criticize, construct, gossip, learn, hate and love by narrative' (Hardy 1968, p. 5). Another literary scholar, Peter Brooks, declared in the 1980s that '[o]ur lives are ceaselessly intertwined with narrative, with the stories that we tell and hear told, those we dream or imagine or would like to tell, all of which are reworked in that story of our own lives that we narrate to ourselves in an episodic, sometimes semiconscious, but virtually uninterrupted monologue' (Brooks 1984, p. 3). It is worth noting that the rise of the story in humanistic and social sciences succeeds the long literary theoretical discussion on the 'death of the novel' that includes claims about the novel's experiential obsolescence in the modern world. The religious studies scholar Ted Estess, for one, remarked in the 1970s that '[i]t is deeply ironic that while some humanists engage in a concerted effort to resurrect the metaphor of story as a way of understanding the deepest matters of human existence, many literary artists speak of the death of the novel and despair over the story-form itself' (Estess 1974, p. 416).
3. Turner 1996, preface. The philosopher Louis O. Mink calls narrative 'a primary and irreducible form of human comprehension' (Mink 2001, p. 214). For another philosopher, C. G. Prado, we are 'natural story-tellers long before we are Aristotelian rational beings' (Prado 1984, p. 136). The communication theorist Walter Fisher (1987), in turn, claims that human *reasoning* is narrative in form.
4. Turner 1996, pp. 4–5; emphasis added.
5. MacIntyre 2007, pp. 211 and 215–18.
6. Dennett 1988, p. 1029. MacIntyre, for his part, thinks that we are never more than 'co-authors' of our narratives, as we cannot decide the 'plot'

of our life by ourselves (see MacIntyre 2007, p. 213). The psychologist David Polkinghorne is more modest: we are narrators, not authors, of our 'self-stories', as 'we do not control all the circumstances that affect the outcome of those stories' (Polkinghorne 1991, p. 146). The philosopher David J. Velleman (2005, p. 58) states that 'we invent ourselves [. . .] but we really are the characters whom we invent'. The philosopher Marya Schechtman thinks that we should look at our self-narratives from the point of view of a character, author and critic, see Schechtman (2011, pp. 413–15). Shaun Gallagher (2015, p. 141) concludes his analysis on 'being a novelist' by saying that artistry requires imaginative effort beyond everyday storytelling.

7 Glover 1988, p. 152. See, however, Glover's various insights on contingency, limits, selection, abridgement and editing (wishful thinking, fantasy, self-deception), and the like in inner storytelling, in Glover 1988, ch. 14.

8 Bruner 1991, p. 5; elsewhere, Bruner maintains that '[i]n the end, we *become* the autobiographical narratives by which we "tell about" our lives' (Bruner 1987, p. 15; emphasis in original).

9 Bruner 2003, p. 89.

10 Kreiswirth 2000, p. 311; Phelan 2005, p. 206.

11 See, for example, Livingston 2009, pp. 25–36.

12 Lamarque 2014, pp. 63–4.

13 Lamarque 2014, p. 64.

14 Lamarque 2014, p. 64.

15 See Barthes 1980, p. 123.

16 Goldie 2012, p. 148.

17 Strawson 2004, p. 443.

18 Strawson 2004, p. 447. For criticism of the psychological support which Strawson cites for his claim, see Eakin 2006, p. 184.

19 Strawson 2004, p. 448. Crispin Sartwell, for one, claims that we may become trapped in our narratives, being unable to live in the present, see Sartwell 2000, chs. 1 and 2.

20 Levi 1989, pp. 23–4.

21 Shils 1981, p. 51.

22 Novitz (2001, p. 115) aptly remarks that even introspection is not just about remembering. Rather, Novitz points out that what we can recall about our past depends greatly on the questions we ask ourselves, whereas the questions depend on our purposes in asking them; purposes, in turn, are largely shaped by social influences.
23 See Zahavi 2007, pp. 181–2. See also Bruner 2003, pp. 65–6 and 69.
24 The philosopher Anthony Kerby goes on to argue that '[t]he individual is in fact something of a chameleon, adapting itself very much to the needs of the moment' (Kerby 1991, p. 64; cf. p. 47).
25 See Kerby 1991, p. 90.
26 See Bruner 2003, pp. 13–15.
27 Respectively, we might take an author's undue sincerity and openness, or her insisting on telling the truth about a difficult matter, as a signal of a partial and coloured account, making us eager to hear the other side of the story – or simply making us uninterested in the truth of the account.
28 Lamarque 2014, p. 166. For Lamarque's detailed view of opacity in literature, see Lamarque 2014, ch. 8.
29 See Lamarque 2014, p. viii.
30 Lamarque 2014, pp. viii–ix.
31 Lamarque 2014, p. ix.
32 Lamarque 2014, p. 68. Lamarque (2014) remarks that the general knowledge of iconic characters is very poor and contains merely the basic facts; in the cultural mainstream the characters are 'bare abstractions' and their literary origins irrelevant or unknown. Lamarque thinks that while such 'impoverished knowledge' is valuable in providing means to locate the characters in cultural mythology, it can provide only trivial analogues between literature and life.
33 Goodman 1978, p. 103; see also p. 104.
34 Danto 1981, pp. 172, 173; emphasis in original.
35 Lamarque 2014, p. 68. However, when praising the richness of art, we ought not to forget the colourfulness of everyday events, the meaningful tones and nuances in ordinary conversation, gestures and facial expressions. Indeed, one could argue that no *textual* presentation

can ever reach the complexity of everyday (multisensuous) human encounters. Analogues between life and non-literary narrative arts have also been made (see, for example, Randall 2014, pp. 112–13). It is, however, plausible to expect that analogies with other art forms will bring along new medium-specific issues, while the question of opacity remains. Exploring the pros and cons of these analogues would itself be a topic of a study.

36 Lamarque 2014, p. ix and pp. 78–9. See also Williams 2009, pp. 310–11; Polkinghorne 1991, p. 146.
37 See also Goldie (2012, pp. 161–73) for our 'fictionalizing tendencies', such as plotting out our lives, finding agency where there is none, desiring closure and thinking in terms of genre and character; and Strawson (2004, pp. 441–3) for our tendencies to form-finding, storytelling and revision.
38 Lamarque 2014, p. ix and p. 30.
39 Lamarque 2014, p. 29.
40 Lamarque 2014, pp. 29–30. Cf. Bicknell 2004, p. 415. Our lives might resemble novels, 'but bad ones, cluttered and undisciplined ones', says David Carr (1985, p. 115). Paul Ricœur (1992, p. 160), in turn, reminds one of the distinctive temporality of literary narratives (story/plot distinction, iterativity).
41 Kermode 2000, p. 136. See Roquentin's encounter with the root of the chestnut tree in Sartre's *Nausea*. For 'viscosity', see also Sartre (1943, pp. 646–62).
42 See Goldie 2012, pp. 70–2. Noël Carroll (2007b, pp. 4–5) remarks that we can think of closure as a phenomenological impression of finality; David J. Velleman (2003, pp. 6–7), in turn, identifies closure with emotional resolution.
43 Lamarque 2014, p. 64; see also Bicknell 2004, p. 415.
44 See, for example, chapters in *Beyond Narrative Coherence: An Introduction*, ed. Matti Hyvärinen (2010) and Hyvärinen (2012), pp. 328–30.
45 The idea is rooted in Monika Fludernik's influential, yet challenged definition in which 'narrativity' is constituted by 'experientiality' or

'the quasi-mimetic evocation of "real-life experience"'. For Fludernik, experientiality 'reflects a cognitive schema of embodiedness that relates to human existence and human concerns'. From the definition it follows that 'there can [. . .] be narratives without plot, but there cannot be any narratives without a human (anthropomorphic) experiencer of some sort at some narrative level' (Fludernik 1996, p. 12). Another influential narrative theorist, David Herman, sees narrative as 'a basic human strategy for coming to terms with time, process, and change'; for him, 'stories are accounts of what happened to particular people – and of what it was like for them to experience what happened – in particular circumstances and with specific consequences' (Herman 2007, p. 3). For a survey of recent definitions of narrative, see Marie-Laure Ryan's (2007) excellent overview in the same volume.

46 Freeman 2017, p. 23; emphasis in original.
47 Ricœur 1985, p. 214. Likewise, the critic Roy Pascal (1960, p. 1) claims that 'autobiographies offer an unparalleled insight into the mode of consciousness of other men. Even if what they tell us is not factually true, or only partly true, it always is true evidence of their personality.'
48 Eakin 1985, p. 3; see also Eakin 1999, ch. 2 and 2006, p. 181. For a view of plasticity and procedurality of identities in autobiographical writing, see Löschnigg 2010, p. 262.
49 Kerby 1991, pp. 83 and 89–90.
50 Nonetheless, autobiographies depict events of which many can never be verified; and where there have been witnesses to the reported events, their testimonies are also subject to interpretation and assessment.
51 Cooper 1995, p. 206; Elgin 1996, p. 123, 2007, pp. 35–6.
52 See Cooper 1995, p. 213; Elgin 2002, pp. 3–5.
53 See, for example, Zagzebski 2001, pp. 241 and 244, 2009, pp. 144–5; Kvanvig 2003, pp. 96–7 and 192.
54 See Cooper 1995, p. 206; Elgin 2006, pp. 199–215, 2007, pp. 33–42.
55 This idea is most comprehensively supported by Catherine Elgin, who has forcefully argued that understanding is not factive or indifferent to truth, see, for example, *True Enough*, esp. ch. 2. See also Zagzebski's (2001, p. 245) view of truth as a thin and understanding as a thick epistemic goal.

56 Elgin 2002, p. 11; see also Elgin 2004, p. 131, 2007, p. 38, 2009, pp. 322–30. See also de Regt and Gijsbers's 'How False Theories Can Yield Genuine Understanding' and Le Bihan's 'Enlightening Falsehoods' in *Explaining Understanding*, edited by Grimm, Baumberger and Ammon.
57 Cooper 1995, p. 210.
58 Kvanvig 2003, p. 196.
59 Elgin, 1993, p. 14; Zagzebski 2001, p. 242.
60 See, for example, Elgin 2002, p. 5.
61 Cooper 1995, p. 210.
62 Zagzebski 2001, p. 244. Zagzebski holds that while alternative representations may be better or worse, more than one may be equally good or accurate.
63 Kerby 1991, p. 54; emphasis in original.
64 Polkinghorne 2003, p. 11.
65 See Hutto 2007a, p. 12, b, pp. 52–60; Cooper 1988, p. 165. For the relevance of small stories to personal identity, see also Bamberg and Georgakopoulou (2008) and Bamberg 2017. Yet, it is open to question how much we ought to broaden the concept of narrative. Lamarque (2014, pp. 63, 65), for one, claims that a narrative fragment or a short narrative explanation loses the idea of narrativity and that the explanatory power of minuscule narrative explanations is not due to their *narrativity* but *causal* dimension, for instance. Should we say that one-word sentences, for example, are small narratives in the relevant sense or that they are meaningful as they *connect to* broader cultural narratives or *generate* narratives? If everything is narrative and anything can be a narrative, we might want to look for new concepts.
66 The linguists Gillian Brown and George Yule (1983, p. 67) maintain that we humans naturally assume coherence 'in our experience of life in general, hence in our experience of discourse as well'. In turn, the literary scholar Michael Toolan (2009, p. 53) proposes a Gricean-style 'narrative implicature', which maintains that 'the reader of a narrative assumes the general cooperativeness of the teller, and draws on powers of inferencing to fill out the sense of the information conveyed by the teller where these [seem] calculatedly incomplete or indirect'. For

applying Grice's theory of conversational implicature to narratives, see also Bortolussi and Dixon (2003, p. 73) and Nair (2003, ch. 4).

67 See Shils 1981, p. 50. Marya Schechtman (2016, pp. 31–2), in turn, argues that narrative thinking about the self 'allows for a peculiarly human form of self-understanding because of the way in which it enables us to see ourselves as others and so to occupy multiple first-person perspectives at once'. She says that 'When I think about my life as a narrative [...] I see my present perspective as one among many interacting and changing perspectives, all of which are mine. I thus have ironic distance not only from my past and future selves, but from my present self as well. Since I understand my present viewpoint as one among many I will inhabit, there is simultaneously a sense of myself as the subject of the present point of view and as the persisting subject who sees things differently at different times.'

68 See Elgin (2004) for a view of the non-factivity of understanding.

69 Brockmeier and Meretoja 2014, p. 6.

70 Kornblith 2014, p. 25.

71 Charles Taylor (1989, p. 36) writes: 'Even as the most independent adult, there are moments when I cannot clarify what I feel until I talk about it with certain special partner(s), who know me, or have wisdom, or with whom I have an affinity. [...] This is the sense in which one cannot be a self on one's own.' According to Taylor, 'The full definition of someone's identity [...] usually involves not only his stand on moral and spiritual matters but also some reference to a defining community.'

72 In addition to Polkinghorne, see Goldie (2012, p. 2) and Gregory Currie (2007, pp. 174 and 176–7).

73 Goldie 2012, p. 56.

74 Goldie 2012, p. 62.

75 Zamir 2019, p. 1.

76 Ricœur 1990, p. 75.

77 See French (2001) for a literary-philosophical exploration of vengeance.

78 See Lamarque 2014, pp. 149, 151.

79 Goldie 2012, p. 151.

Chapter 4

1. Woolf 1996, p. 31.
2. McHale 1987, p. 9.
3. Palmer 2011, p. 276.
4. Herman 2011, p. 264.
5. Hamburger 1993, p. 83; emphasis removed; Hamburger 1968, p. 73.
6. Cohn 1999, p. 106.
7. Ryan 1991, p. 67.
8. Fludernik 1996, p. 48.
9. Here are Willems and Jacobs: 'Engaging with fiction is a natural and rich behavior, providing a unique window onto the mind and brain, particularly for mental simulation, emotion, empathy, and immersion' (Willems and Jacobs 2016, p. 243).
10. Zunshine 2006, p. 5. In addition to competing models of ToM (theory-theory vs. simulation theory), it is disputed whether interpersonal understanding includes ToM.
11. See Currie 2016a.
12. Palmer 2004, p. 12.
13. Palmer 2004, p. 10. Palmer (Palmer 2004, p. 246) remarks that much of our knowledge about fictional minds are hypotheses and conjectures which we base on the characters' actions.
14. Palmer 2010, p. 9. Palmer does not claim that fictional minds are identical to real minds; rather, he thinks that fictional minds are semiotic constructs that are similar to real minds (Palmer 2010, p. 19).
15. Palmer 2011, p. 275.
16. Herman 2011, pp. 253–4.
17. Joshua Gang (2013, p. 117), who questions the idea of the 'inward turn' in modernism, aptly remarks that '[m]odernism was not psychologically monolithic; instead, an array of psychological theories – including behaviorism, structuralism and psychoanalysis – circulated simultaneously and competed against each other'.
18. See, for example, Meisel 2007, esp. ch. 4. Virginia Woolf's interests in theories of knowledge and language are also well known. For the

connections between her literary work and philosophical theories of her time, see, for example, Hintikka 1979; Banfield 2000; and Quigley 2008.

19 Woolf 2008, p. 8.
20 Woolf 2008, p. 9. According to Woolf, modern writers' interest 'lies very likely in the dark places of psychology. At once, therefore, the accent falls a little differently; the emphasis is upon something hitherto ignored; at once a different outline of form becomes necessary, difficult for us to grasp, incomprehensible to our predecessors' (Woolf 2008, p. 11).
21 The alleged cognitive value of modernist narratives ought not to be identified with their ability to reveal individual minds. Modernist narratives illuminate a cultural understanding of the world, as Auerbach remarks in his chapter on Woolf. A related view involves looking at how Joyce's *Finnegans Wake* reflects the scientific understanding of his time, a world view affected by psychoanalysis and quantum physics, for instance.
22 Auerbach 1953, p. 552.
23 Woolf 1978, p. 207.
24 Suzette Henke, cited from Alber 2011, p. 221.
25 Alber 2011, p. 220; emphasis added.
26 Fludernik 2003, p. 256.
27 See, for example, Heider and Simmel 1944.
28 The critics point out, for instance, that the subjective experience which a literary work gives rise to does not represent a form of knowledge; that the cognitivist theories do not distinguish between genuine and putative knowledge nor provide means for distinguishing between what is true or false; and that the theories do not demonstrate an intrinsic link between literary response and learning (Lamarque and Olsen 1994, p. 371). Further, Lamarque and Olsen argue that 'it is most unlikely that literary works taken as a whole – as *works* – will present situations that could provide a coherent and unified experience describable as "knowing what it is like"' (Lamarque and Olsen 1994, p. 378; emphasis in original). Further, they argue that a

'Hamlet-situation, for example, is far too complex and specific to give rise to any single and sustained experience of this kind, certainly not one that will be relevant to a reader's daily life' (Lamarque and Olsen 1994, p. 378).
29. Harold 2016, p. 390; emphasis in original.
30. See Lamarque and Olsen 1994, pp. 261–5.
31. In this book and philosophical aesthetics in general, 'cognitivism' means the view which holds that artworks can provide their audiences significant knowledge and insight concerning matters of human interest. The position should not be confused with the cognitive scientific study of literature.
32. Lamarque and Olsen 1994, p. 145. Akin to Walton, Lamarque and Olsen also emphasize the value of the dual standpoint. They (Lamarque and Olsen 1994, p. 144) think that '[b]eing "caught up" in fictional worlds and at the same time recognizing their fictionality involves a delicate balance – even a tension – which certainly accounts for much of the pleasure and value of imaginative works of art'.
33. Lamarque and Olsen 1994, p. 146.
34. Lamarque 2014, p. ix; emphasis in original.
35. When drawing, say, a philosophically interesting setting or insight from fiction, there is the question of its worldly extension. Lamarque and Olsen (1994, p. 454) maintain that abstract ideas in literature are based on the narrator's perspectival descriptions and essentially connected with the fictional particulars and that transferring the ideas to another context – the world – trivializes them.
36. The literary critic Maria Mäkelä (2013), for one, argues that literary narratives never reveal their characters' minds; rather, literary works foreground and thematize the telling and hide the underlying experience. In her view, literature is characteristically ambiguous, seemingly objective descriptions turn out to be subjective, and the origin of a thought in fiction always remains vague.
37. Cohn 1978, p. 44. Representation is, of course, tied to artistic conventions. As Cohn puts it, '[t]he monologues of *Ulysses* may be regarded as particularly clear instances of the historical dimension

of realism Roman Jakobson defined in his essay "On Realism in Art": the revolutionary artist deforms the existing artistic canons for the sake of closer imitation of reality; the conservative public misunderstands the deformation of the canon as a distortion of reality. The first generation of *Ulysses* readers, conditioned by a long tradition of monologues modeled on dialogues, could only have experienced Bloom's and Stephen's mental productions as radical departures from realistic representation. [. . .] Today's reader is more likely than his grandparents to take Joyce's conception of verbal thought for granted, to accept the notion that it differs from communicative speech in a number of significant respects, and to accept the monologues of *Ulysses* as supremely convincing achievements of formal mimeticism' (Cohn 1978, pp. 92–3).

38 Anderson 2017, p. 255; emphasis in original.
39 Anderson 2017, p. 240; emphasis in original.
40 Anderson 2017, p. 240; emphasis in original.
41 Lamarque 2014, p. 38.
42 See, for example, Greene 1938, 1940.
43 Stace and Greene 1938, p. 656; emphasis added.
44 According to Stace, art has 'real significance in the light of man' (Stace and Greene 1938, p. 656). Yet, he maintains that art's contribution to *truth* is to be understood in terms of 'propositions and the ordinary judgments of the intellect' (Stace and Greene 1938, p. 656).
45 Walsh 1943, p. 433; emphasis added. Likewise, in 1984 Mary Mothersill wrote: 'It is true that works of art depict or describe the world, express thoughts and emotions, and contribute to moral enlightenment, and there is no reason why, individually or collectively, they should not be judged in the light of established standards. The difficulty is that, in such a light, the arts make a poor showing: as a means of acquiring new truths about the worlds or the soul, they are in competition with the sciences and with philosophy. [. . .] The advocates of such views are therefore driven to qualify their respective theses: the knowledge that we gain from art is not ordinary knowledge, not to be considered as a species of "justified true belief"' (Mothersill 1984, p. 4).

46 For exceptions, see introduction in Mikkonen 2013.
47 Altieri 1981, p. 271.
48 Wood 2005, pp. 11–12.
49 While the distinction between knowledge and understanding is not clear and evident for philosophers nor for cognitive psychologists, for instance, it is widely recognized in everyday parlance and seems to capture some epistemic distinction we make between knowledge and knowledge-structures or some other higher-order knowledge. For example, in *How to Read a Book* the philosopher and educator Mortimer J. Adler and the writer Charles Van Doren make a distinction between *reading for information* and *reading for understanding*. They explain: 'The poorer reader is usually able to do only the first sort of reading: for information. The better reader can do that, of course, and more. He can increase his understanding as well as his store of facts.' When a work increases a reader's understanding, it does not merely provide her new facts but also 'throw[s] a new and perhaps more revealing light on *all* the facts he knows' (Adler and Van Doren 1972, p. 9; emphasis in original).
50 Baumberger, Beisbart and Brun 2016.
51 Goodman and Elgin 1988; Elgin 1996, 2006.
52 Grimm 2012, p. 103. A focal issue in the study of understanding concerns the nature of 'grasping'.
53 These views have been called 'theories of conceptual enrichment' (Lamarque and Olsen 1994, p. 378), 'theories of cognitive strengthening' (Lamarque 2009, p. 250), and 'neo-cognitivism' (Gibson 2008, p. 580). These views generally draw on the idea that literary works may show us what it is like to be a certain kind of person or in a certain kind of situation, adding that such virtual experience contributes to the reader's understanding of concepts (say, what 'loneliness' is about).
54 Murdoch 1993; Elgin 1993; Carroll 1998.
55 Reid 1969; Beardsmore 1971; Putnam 1979; Hagberg 1994; Graham 2000; A. Pettersson 2011.
56 Gibson 2007, pp. 111, 116.
57 Novitz 1987, p. 137.

58 For Carroll (1998, p. 143), understanding is a capacity to manipulate what we know and to apply it intelligibly and appropriately; 'to see and to be responsive to connections between our beliefs'. In his view, the deepening of understanding is 'more a matter of grasping the significance of the connections between antecedently possessed knowledge'.
59 Carroll 1998, pp. 140 and 142.
60 Carroll 1998, p. 142.
61 Similarly, Elgin remarks that works of fiction may provide their readers with *new categories*, such as that of 'whitewoman' in Toni Morrison's *Beloved* (Elgin 1996, pp. 186–7).
62 Novitz 1987, pp. 119–20.
63 Wilson 2004, p. 327.
64 Bruner 1991, p. 12.
65 See Fludernik 2003, p. 256. Fludernik (1996, p. 172) claims that '[b]y the time of Joyce's and Woolf's depiction of minds in their plenitude, these authors could build on cognitive parameters which were well in place and available for use: readers had considerable training in tuning in on such non-natural mind reading within a natural frame'.
66 Alber 2011, p. 211.
67 Alber 2011, p. 227. 'Unnatural' may be taken to include the so-called omniscient narrators and other elements that are present in 'realist' narratives too.
68 Alber 2009, p. 82.
69 Alber 2009, pp. 82–3, 91–3; see also Alber 2011, pp. 222–4.
70 Alber 2011, p. 232; emphasis added.
71 See Elgin 1996, p. 192; Zamir 2007, p. 66.
72 Nussbaum 1990, p. 46.
73 Nussbaum 1990, p. 47.
74 Of course, a literary work may be both complex and promote a given view. There is naturally a great deal of shared understanding of fictional events, reasons that fictional characters have for their actions, and, say, ethical positions which works take. Many interpretative disputes stem from theoretical standpoints and concern the

significance given for fictional events. And some interpretations are of course more plausible, more interesting, more illuminating and more rewarding than some others.

75 Kundera 1999, p. 18.
76 The common argument against the idea of literary works as thought-experiments, for instance, is that they do not make univocal claims (for recent views, see Cave 2016, p. 143 and Huemer 2019).
77 Lamarque 2010b, p. 382.
78 While *ambiguity* or abundance of meaning is generally praised as an artistic merit, *obscurity* or deficiency of meaning is seldom considered meritorious (see Stanford 1972, p. 73).
79 Here, see, for example, T. Pettersson (2002) and Goldman (2013, esp. ch I.3).
80 Posner 1997, p. 12.
81 Posner 1997, p. 12.
82 Posner 1998, p. 409.
83 Indeed, Monroe C. Beardsley (1981, p. 163) wished for 'a classification of the factors in literature that make for obscurity, and hence of the types of obscurity'.
84 Literary critic Päivi Mehtonen (2003) suggests that there is a whole tradition of 'Heraclitean obscurantism' in the history of philosophy. In her view, the tradition includes philosophers such as Schleiermacher, Hegel, Nietzsche and Heidegger.
85 Harrison 1991, p. 50.
86 Harrison 1991, p. 50.
87 Harrison 1991, p. 4.
88 Harrison 1991, p. 6.
89 John 1998, p. 340.
90 John 1998, p. 340.
91 John 1998, p. 337; emphasis in original.
92 John 1998, p. 340.
93 Novitz 1987, p. 139.
94 Novitz 2004, p. 992. Here, one can observe how cognitivists may defend art's epistemic value with various claims: artworks can have

epistemic value in both clarifying our concepts and problematizing our conceptions.

95 Elgin 2002, p. 12.
96 Davis 2013, p. 129.
97 Davis 2013, p. 139.
98 Davis 2013, p. 139.
99 Elgin argues that 'fictions sensitize us to delicate differences in degree, demeanor, and detail that affect moral standing. *If they thereby make moral deliberation more demanding, they also make moral judgment more acute*' (Elgin 1996, p. 186; emphasis added).
100 See Derrida 1972, pp. 295–301, 1982, pp. 247–52.
101 In his classic study, William Empson (1965, p. 235) puts it thus: 'An ambiguity [. . .] is not satisfying in itself, nor is it, considered as a device on its own, a thing to be attempted; it must in each case arise from, and be justified by, the peculiar requirements of the situation. On the other hand, it is a thing which the more interesting and valuable situations are more likely to justify.'
102 We could speak of confusion caused by syntactic obscurity, semantic obscurity, narrative or structural obscurity and thematic obscurity, to mention some. This chapter discusses confusion understood as thematic obscurity in which the story is clear but its thematic meaning is not.
103 In modernist literature, obscurity became a positive tenet, 'constitutive of the very being of the art work', as Allon White (1981, p. 16) puts it. Terry Eagleton (2012, p. 185), in turn, says that modern literature is ambiguous 'because it turns in on itself, troubled by the absence of an assured audience, and takes itself as its subject in a way that shuts it off from any easy access from outside; because it seeks to distil something of the fragmentation and ambiguity of modern existence, qualities which invade its form and language and risk rendering it opaque; because it turns its back contemptuously on the political, commercial, technical and bureaucratic discourses around it, which it feels are transparent only at the cost of being degraded, and seeks for itself a thicker, more subtle and elusive idiom; because it wants to avoid being

treated as a commodity, and uses its obscurity as a way of preventing itself from being too easily consumed.'

104 Phillips 1982, p. 9.
105 Winch 1972, p. 154.
106 Putnam 1978, p. 87. Likewise, Noël Carroll (1998, p. 148) acknowledges that some literary works present moral problems that 'appear not to be satisfactorily resolvable' and suggests that this 'seems to enrich moral understanding by stretching its reflective resources as one struggles to imagine a livable course of action'.
107 It has also been proposed that literary works, considered as thought-experiments, expose 'hidden motives and feelings of the agent' better than philosophers' examples (Carroll 2002, pp. 18–19), and that by representing extreme cases, literary works may reveal aspects that are not paid attention in philosophical inquiries (see Elgin 1993, p. 26, 2007, p. 50).
108 Gaut 2007, p. 162. Gaut also discusses an irresolvable moral dilemma presented in William Styron's novel *Sophie's Choice* (1979).
109 Often, however, the author's stance towards such assertions is unclear. Indeed, Terry Eagleton (2012, p. 152) remarks that authors 'may want their readers to half believe that what they say is true, which is what Richardson may have meant by his comments on *Clarissa*'. This is one of the peculiarities of fiction. An author may simultaneously make an assertion and pull it back; she is not responsible for the claims she includes or represents in her work, and yet she may express them.
110 See, for example, Aristotle, *Rhetoric* 1407b.
111 Lamarque and Olsen 1994, p. 409.
112 Lamarque and Olsen 1994, p. 384.
113 John 1998, p. 341.
114 John 1998, p. 342. See also John's (1998, pp. 341–2) discussion on the genre's role in constraining concepts used in a work.
115 Haaparanta 2019.
116 See Elgin (2002, p. 9) on the 'simple goodness' of Alyosha Karamazov, Iago's 'unadulterated evil' and Captain Ahab's 'blind obsession'.

117 Currie (2007, p. 173) thinks that '[i]t is sometimes a mark of quality in a fictional narrative that it helps us to adopt, in imagination, a point of view that is not merely different from our own, but alien to it in some ways. We may see that as morally enlarging, either because it reveals merit in a point of view to which we were previously insensitive, or because it helps us to understand, from the inside, the attractions of a distorted way of seeing things.' Likewise, Robert Stecker (2003) compares literary works to those philosophical works which ultimately *fail* in argumentation but which we still value as they clarify our thinking and function as instruments in truth-seeking.

118 Stace and Greence 1938, p. 658.

119 Putnam 1978, p. 89.

120 Stolnitz 1992, p. 191.

121 Lamarque 1997, pp. 19–20.

122 Pouivet 2011, p. 16.

123 Alber 2009, p. 93.

124 Alber 2011, p. 227.

125 See Lamarque 2009, p. 250; Currie 2014b, p. 443.

Chapter 5

1 Lamarque 1997, p. 20. Elsewhere, Lamarque (2019) wonders if readers who respond emotionally to fictions exhibit high degrees of empathy, as great many theories and empirical studies of reading suggest. He answers that 'anecdotally there is no strong evidence that literary academics or teachers are more empathetic than academics in other areas or members of the public at large', whereas so-called ordinary readers 'are simply too diffuse a group, sociologically, psychologically, or in terms of age, education, interests, or disposition, to promise any kind of coherent empirical result'.

2 See Zamir 2007, pp. 17–18.

3 Feagin 1997, p. 97; emphasis in original.

4 Robinson 2005, p. 193.
5 Currie 2014b, p. 437.
6 Currie 2014b, pp. 438–9.
7 Currie 2014b, p. 447.
8 Currie 2014b, pp. 446 and 447. For criticism of the lack of evidence in literary theory, see also Martindale (1996) and Posner (1997, pp. 9–10).
9 For instance, it is not clear whether David Novitz is describing a practice or rather suggesting a way of reading in saying that the '[r]eaders of *Anna Karenina* do not only imagine or re-create the heroine's quandaries, but given sufficient interest, they actually ponder and explore them. They imagine what it is like to be assailed by such problems, they feel the fright and despair that accompany them, and, arguably as a result, they are able to discern their overwhelming complexity' (Novitz 1987, p. 135).
10 As the philosopher Richard Eldridge (2009, p. 13) puts it, the problem of philosophy of literature is that '[i]t seeks to understand the work of literature too readily against the background of protocols of knowing that were developed principally within the epistemology of the natural sciences, thus all but inevitably casting literature as secondary, derivative, decorative, or deficient'.
11 Wilson 2004, p. 327.
12 See Currie 2010, p. 116.
13 See Gerrig and Prentice 1991; Prentice, Gerrig and Bailis 1997; Prentice and Gerrig 1999; Wheeler, Green and Brock 1999; Marsh, Meade and Roediger 2003; Marsh and Fazio 2006; Butler, Dennis and Marsh 2012. According to these studies, readers of fiction may be vulnerable to false information, as information in fictions is not assessed as critically as in persuasive communication. See, however, Stacie Friend's (2014) insightful scrutiny of these studies.
14 Green and Brock 2000, 2002; Gerrig and Rapp 2004.
15 Appel and Richter 2007.
16 Gerrig and Rapp 2004; Mar et al. 2006; Mar and Oatley 2008; Mar, Oatley and Peterson 2009; Johnson 2012; Johnson et al. 2013; Kidd

and Castano 2013a; Bal and Veltkamp 2013; Djikic, Oatley and Moldoveanu 2013a; Tamir et al. 2016; Dodell-Feder and Tamir 2018; see also Mar 2018a.
17 Djikic et al. 2009; Djikic, Oatley and Carland 2012; Djikic and Oatley 2014.
18 Kuiken, Miall and Sikora 2004.
19 Hakemulder 2000.
20 Mar, Peskin and Fong 2010.
21 Djikic, Oatley and Moldoveanu 2013b.
22 Miall 2000.
23 Kidd and Castano 2013a, p. 379. There has been much scrutiny in psychology and elsewhere of this study; both negative and positive replication attempts, Kidd and Castano's further research, and discussion on the original research and studies that followed it. For a follow-up, see Kidd, Ongis and Castano 2016; for replication and failed replication, see, for example, Pino and Mazza 2016; van Kuijk et al. 2018; Kidd and Castano 2017; 2018a, b; Samur, Tops and Koole 2018; Camerer et al. 2018; Panero et al. 2016, and 2017.
24 Stock 2014, p. 205.
25 Earlier research has often used stories specifically produced for the study. In Johnson's experiment, for instance, the 'story was designed to induce compassionate feelings for the characters and model prosocial behavior'. Contemporary research prefers literary works proper – short stories or chapters of novels. There are, of course, practical limitations as for the length of the material. However, some researchers acknowledge that the experience of a novel might be different than reading a single chapter of it (see, for example, Bal and Veltkamp 2013, p. 10).
26 See Bal and Veltkamp 2013, p. 9; Koopman and Hakemulder 2015, pp. 80, 88.
27 Kidd and Castano 2013b.
28 Koopman and Hakemulder 2015, p. 88; Hakemulder, Fialho and Bal 2016, p. 21; Polvinen 2017, p. 137.
29 Panero et al. 2016, p. e53.

30 See, for example, Kidd and Castano 2013a, p. 378.
31 For such a view, see, for example, Miall 1994. Miall and Kuiken (1999, p. 123) maintain that 'literariness is constituted when stylistic or narrative variations strikingly defamiliarize conventionally understood referents and prompt reinterpretive transformations of a conventional concept or feeling'.
32 Djikic et al. 2009; see Oatley 1994, 1999, p. 109, 2011, p. 160, 2016; Mar and Oatley 2008.
33 Caracciolo and van Duuren 2015, p. 527; see Hakemulder 2000.
34 Bal, Butterman and Bakker 2011, p. 367.
35 Bal, Butterman and Bakker 2011, p. 367.
36 Fong, Mullin and Mar 2013, p. 371.
37 Fong, Mullin and Mar 2013, p. 373.
38 Panero et al. 2016, p. e52.
39 Koopman 2015, p. 65; Koopman and Hakemulder 2015, p. 86; Panero et al. 2016, pp. e52–e53.
40 Richell et al. 2003.
41 See, for example, Koopman 2015, pp. 63–4; see also Koopman and Hakemulder 2015, pp. 86–7.
42 Panero et al. 2016, e53.
43 Currie 2016c, p. 55.
44 Currie 2016c, p. 57. Currie (2016c, p. 55) criticizes the basing of moral cognition and behaviour on empathy in claiming that '[h]elping behaviour produced by unreflective empathy tends to be arbitrarily disposed, favours those close to us with whom we empathise easily, and proceeds without regard to justice or economy of means; it makes us sensitive to the individual victim of a policy and indifferent to the many whose lives the policy saved'.
45 Black and Barnes 2015, p. 10. It is also difficult to separate reading and the role of discussion or reflection prompted by certain kind of studies that are after the reader's literary experience (see Keen 2007, p. 92; Hakemuelder, Fialho and Bal 2016).
46 Panero et al. 2016, pp. e52–e53. If we could study real readers in their 'natural habitat', it would be interesting to see what all there is

in the social practice of literature that contributes to the assumed impact of reading (discussions on books, newspaper criticism, author interviews, etc.).
47 See, for example, Graesser, Olde and Klettke 2002, p. 230.
48 Fludernik 2009, p. 19.
49 For classical defences of this view, see Culler (1981) and Bourdieu (1984).
50 Miall 2008, p. 320.
51 Miall 2006, p. 293; see also Miall 2005, p. 142.
52 Fludernik 2009, p. 19.
53 Mar et al. 2006, p. 707.
54 Currie 2016c, 58–9.
55 Currie 2014b, p. 444. Mar (2018b) proposes guidelines and a research framework for future investigations on how fictional stories might promote social cognition.
56 Currie 2016b, p. 653.
57 For an illustration of – and doubt in – explaining interpretation in terms of schemas and scripts, see, for example, Gerrig 1991, pp. 32–3 and Gerrig and Egidi 2003, pp. 40–1. For another illustration, see Bortolussi and Dixon 2003, pp. 111–18.
58 Alber et al. 2010, p. 114.
59 Alber 2009, p. 80.
60 See Alber et al. 2012, pp. 371–82.
61 For an illuminating philosophical take on the advancement of a mechanic's experiential understanding of engines, see Crawford (2009).
62 Isenberg 1987, p. 128; emphasis in original.
63 See Shusterman 1989, p. 7.
64 Kathleen Stock and Katherine Thomson-Jones, for instance, remark that analytic aestheticians today are critical of the 'narrow analytic program' of the pioneering analytic aestheticians. As they observe, the scope of aesthetics today is broader and more diverse than the mere analysis of concepts and principles. Questions in metaphysics and the philosophy of mind are also given much

attention in contemporary aesthetics. See Stock and Thomson-Jones 2008, p. xii.
65 See Beardsley 1958, pp. 3–7.
66 Lamarque 2009, p. 7; see also Olsen 1987, pp. 199–201.
67 Carroll 2009, p. 1.
68 Ross 2012, p. 363.
69 Lamarque and Olsen 1994, pp. 332–3. Some philosophers have, however, argued that critics do explicate implicit theses in literary works, and that it is the task of general readers to evaluate the theses, see, for example, Kivy 1995, pp. 122, 125; see also Carroll 2009, p. 56. Some others have argued that certain critical terms, such as 'profundity' and 'psychological plausibility' have a conceptual connection with truthfulness, see Rowe (1997, p. 379) and Currie (2012, pp. 28–30).
70 Felski 2008, p. 25.
71 Matz 2006, p. 215.
72 Miller 2008, pp. 5 and ix.
73 Jones 1992, pp. i, ii.
74 Jones 1992, p. iv.
75 Jones 1992, p. i.
76 Carroll 2002, p. 10.
77 Carroll 2002, p. 15; see also Kivy 1997, pp. 20–1.
78 Carroll 2002, p. 15.
79 John 1998, p. 331.
80 Lamarque 2009, p. 254.
81 Lamarque 2009, p. 250.
82 See, for example, Rose 1992.
83 See, for example, Julian W. Connolly's account of critics' and common readers' (early) responses to the work, including the reactions of Nietzsche, Zweig, Hesse, Freud and Mann, in Connolly 2013, ch. 5.
84 See, for example, Miesen 2003; Charlton, Burbaum and Pette 2004. For an overview and analysis of these sort of studies, see A. Pettersson (2012, pp. 171–80).
85 This I have learnt from the sociologist Matti Hyvärinen.

86 Hakemulder (2000, p. 31) remarks that reader reports might rather reflect humanistic assumptions about literature than its actual influence.
87 Zagzebski 2001, p. 246.
88 Let us not forget the problem of inarticulateness. As Currie (2014b, pp. 446–7) sees it, the cognitive content of a literary work cannot be explicated, for cognitivists themselves maintain that it is not propositional. This claim could be objected to by remarking that articulations of a work's cognitive content could be seen rather as *descriptions* than *paraphrases* of (a part of) that content; that they are not intended to capture the 'cognitive content' of the work but to allude to it, and that the reader is expected to realize the insights herself in reading the work in the way suggested by the philosopher.
89 Foreman-Peck 1983, p. 58.
90 Mill [1873] 2009, p. 98.
91 Malcolm [1958] 2001, p. 95.
92 von Wright 2001, p. 267. The author's translation.
93 Some philosophers working on the concept of understanding have recently argues that objectual understanding comes with a distinctive *feeling*. Jonathan Kvanvig, for one, thinks that 'It is the perceived achievement of objectual understanding [. . .] that produces the "aha" and "eureka" experiences that provide closure of investigation into the subject at hand. [. . .] [I]t is the same thing that is the target of enquiry, since what we are after is the kind of thing that provides and legitimates such closure of enquiry. It is the putting of the pieces of the intellectual puzzle together that does that, and thus it is plausible to contrast the idea that knowledge is the goal of enquiry with the claim that it is objectual understanding instead' (Kvanvig 2011, p. 89). Kvanvig thinks that it is the putting of the pieces of the intellectual puzzle together that produces the feeling and, further, that the feeling suggests that the goal of epistemic enquiry is not knowledge but objectual understanding. Elsewhere, he writes that 'organized elements of thought [explanatory relationships] provide intrinsically satisfying closure to the process of inquiry, yielding a sense or feeling

of completeness to our grasp of a particular subject matter' (Kvanvig 2003, p. 202). While such a feeling is characteristic of our epistemic progress, it might not tell us much about the nature of epistemic enquiry; rather, it may simply stem from relief from anxiety, as we have worked hard on a problem and then solved it.

94 Baxter 1997, p. 63.
95 Ylikoski 2009, p. 105.
96 Currie 2014c, p. 45.
97 Currie 2013; see also Currie 2016a. Hakemulder (2000, p. 31), in turn, reminds us about the distorting character of memory: 'Subjects in self-report studies may be sincere in their self-observations, but their personal reconstruction of their past experiences and the formative effect of these on their character may not always be reliable and is scarcely verifiable.'
98 Sometimes literature is seen as valuable in this enterprise. For example, the critic Jens Brockmeier thinks that literature may help us to see, how understanding is limited, how it intertwines with nonunderstanding and misunderstanding and how it often simply *fails*. He says that '[e]ven if understanding fails, it still can afford a sort of meta-understanding of our limits, about what cannot be understood, and why not' (Brockmeier 2016, p. 94). Of course, in order for failed understanding to be epistemically valuable, we need to *know* that our understanding is failed, so there is dependence on knowledge here. And if we understand *what* we cannot understand and *why*, it seems that we possess *knowledge*.
99 See Lamarque 2009, p. 248.
100 Culler 1975, p. 258.
101 Iser 1987, p. 23.
102 Gibson 2008, p. 575; emphasis in original.
103 Lamarque (Lamarque 2016) demonstrates how it is difficult to infer even *fictional facts* from literary narratives. Did Jane love Rochester in Brontë's *Jane Eyre*? The matter is complicated.
104 Pettersson 2016, p. 239.
105 Posner 1997, p. 20; emphasis in original. Further, people may have expectations about the attitudes or views they think that given works

proclaim. Cultural artefacts are bricks from which identities are constructed. First, there might be one's desire to be a certain kind of person and then the tool, a fiction.

106 Lamarque 2012, p. 79.
107 Lamarque 2012, p. 79; see also Lamarque 2014, pp. 166–7.
108 Cooper 1995, p. 214.
109 Elgin 1996, p. 195.
110 See, for example, Stolnitz 1992.
111 Another reason for the cognitivists' bold claims about artistic cognition might be the reason that 'artistic knowledge' does not cumulate like scientific knowledge; thus, the cognitive 'payoff' of reading a novel is expected to be unforgettable.
112 See Ichino and Currie 2016.

References

Addison, J. ([1712] 1965), *The Spectator, Vol. III*, ed. with an Introduction and Notes by D. F. Bond. Oxford: Clarendon Press.

Adler, M. J. and C. Van Doren ([1940] 1972), *How to Read a Book*. Revised and Updated edition. New York: Simon and Schuster.

Alber, J. (2009), 'Impossible Storyworlds – and What to Do with Them', *StoryWorlds: A Journal of Narrative Studies*, 1: 79–96.

Alber, J. (2011), 'The Ethical Implications of Unnatural Scenarios', in J. Alber, S. Iversen, Louise Brix Jacobsen, Rikke Andersen Kraglund, Henrik Skov Nielsen and Camilla Møhring Reestorff (eds), *Why Study Literature?* 211–33. Aarhus: Aarhus University Press.

Alber, J., S. Iversen, H. S. Nielsen and B. Richardson (2010), 'Unnatural Narratives, Unnatural Narratology: Beyond Mimetic Models', *Narrative*, 18 (2): 113–36.

Alber, J., S. Iversen, H. S. Nielsen and B. Richardson (2012), 'What Is Unnatural about Unnatural Narratology? A Response to Monika Fludernik', *Narrative*, 20 (3): 371–82.

Almendrala, A., *HuffPost*, 19 July 2016, https://www.huffpost.com/entry/reading-fiction-makes-you-better_n_578d61c6e4b0fa896c3fb833

Altieri, C. (1981), *Act and Quality: A Theory of Literary Meaning and Humanistic Understanding*. Amherst: The University of Massachusetts Press.

Alward, P. (2006), 'Leave Me Out of It: De Re, But Not De Se, Imaginative Engagement with Fiction', *Journal of Aesthetics and Art Criticism*, 64 (4): 451–9.

Anderson, L. R. (2017), 'Is Clarissa Dalloway Special?', *Philosophy and Literature*, 4 (1A): 233–71.

Appel, M. and T. Richter (2007), 'Persuasive Effects of Fictional Narratives Increase Over Time', *Media Psychology*, 10 (1): 113–34.

Aristotle ([1924] 2004), *Rhetoric*, trans. W. Rhys Roberts. New York: Dover Publications, Inc.

Auerbach, E. (1953), *Mimesis: The Representation of Reality in Western Literature* [Mimesis: Dargestellte Wirklichkeit in der abendländischen Literatur, 1946], trans. W. R. Trask. Princeton: Princeton University Press.

Austin, J. L. (1975/1962), *How to do Things with Words*, ed. J. O. Urmson and M. Sbisà. Second edition. Oxford: Clarendon Press.

Bal, P. M. and M. Veltkamp (2013), 'How Does Fiction Reading Influence Empathy? An Experimental Investigation on the Role of Emotional Transportation', *PLoS ONE*, 8 (1): e55341. doi:10.1371/journal.pone.0055341

Bal, P. M., O. S. Butterman and A. B. Bakker (2011), 'The Influence of Fictional Narrative Experience on Work Outcomes: A Conceptual Analysis and Research Model', *Review of General Psychology*, 15 (4): 361–70.

Bamberg, M. (2017), 'Stories: Big or Small – Why Do We Care?', in M. Bamberg (ed.), *Narrative: State of the Art*, 165–74. Amsterdam: John Benjamins.

Bamberg, M. and A. Georgakopoulou (2008), 'Small Stories as a New Perspective in Narrative and Identity Analysis', *Text & Talk: An Interdisciplinary Journal of Language, Discourse Communication Studies*, 28: 377–96.

Banfield, A. (2000), *The Phantom Table: Woolf, Fry, Russell and the Epistemology of Modernism*. Cambridge: Cambridge University Press.

Baron-Cohen, S., T. Jolliffe C. Mortimore and M. Robertson (1997), 'Another Advanced Test of Theory of Mind: Evidence from Very High Functioning Adults with Autism or Asperger Syndrome', *The Journal of Child Psychology and Psychiatry*, 38 (7): 813–22.

Baron-Cohen, S., S. Wheelwright J. Hill, Y. Raste, and I. Plumb (2001), 'The "Reading the Mind in the Eyes" Test Revised Version: A Study with Normal Adults, and Adults with Asperger Syndrome or High-functioning Autism', *The Journal of Child Psychology and and Psychiatry*, 2 (2): 241–51.

Barthes, R. ([1974] 2002), *S/Z* [S/Z, 1970], trans. R. Miller. Malden: Blackwell.

Barthes, R. ([1975] 1980), *Roland Barthes par Roland Barthes*. Paris: Seuil.

Baumberger, C., C. Beisbart and G. Brun (2016), 'What Is Understanding? An Overview of Recent Debates in Epistemology and Philosophy of

Science', in S. Grimm, C. Baumberger and S. Ammon (eds), *Explaining Understanding: New Perspectives from Epistemolgy and Philosophy of Science*, 1–34. New York: Routledge.

Baxter, C. (1997), 'Against Epiphanies', in Baxter, *Burning Down the House: Essays on Fiction*, 53–77. Minneapolis: Graywolf Press.

Beardsley, M. C. ([1958] 1981), *Aesthetics: Problems in the Philosophy of Criticism*. Second edition. Indianapolis: Hackett Publishing.

Beardsmore, R. W. (1971), *Art and Morality*. London: Macmillan.

Belluck, P., *The New York Times* blog, 3 October 2013, https://well.blogs.nytimes.com/2013/10/03/i-know-how-youre-feeling-i-read-chekhov/

Beres, D., *Big Think*, 11 September 2017, https://bigthink.com/21st-century-spirituality/reading-rewires-your-brain-for-more-intelligence-and-empathy

Bergado, G., *Mic*, 21 November 2014, https://www.mic.com/articles/104702/science-shows-something-surprising-about-people-who-love-reading-fiction

Bergland, C., *Psychology Today*, 4 January 2014, https://www.psychologytoday.com/us/blog/the-athletes-way/201401/reading-fiction-improves-brain-connectivity-and-function

Bicknell, J. (2004), 'Self-Knowledge and the Limitations of Narrative', *Philosophy and Literature*, 28 (2): 406–16.

Black, J. E. and J. L. Barnes (2015), 'The Effects of Reading Material on Social and Non-Social Cognition', *Poetics*, 52: 32–43.

Booth, W. C. (1988), *The Company We Keep: An Ethics of Fiction*. Chicago: University of Chicago Press.

Bortolussi, M. and P. Dixon (2003), *Psychonarratology: Foundations for the Empirical Study of Literary Response*. Cambridge: Cambridge University Press.

Bourdieu, P. (1984), *Distinction: A Social Critique of the Judgement of Taste* [*La distinction*, 1979], trans. R. Nice. Cambridge, MA: Harvard University Press.

Brinkmann, S. (2017), *Stand Firm. Resisting the Self-Improvement Craze* [Stå fast: et opgør med tidens udviklingstvang, 2014], trans. T. McTurk. Cambridge: Polity Press.

Brockmeier, J. (2016), 'On Failed Understanding', *Storyworlds: A Journal of Narrative Studies*, 8 (1): 77–96.

Brockmeier, J. and H. Meretoja (2014), 'Understanding Narrative Hermeneutics', *StoryWorlds: A Journal of Narrative Studies*, 6: 1–27.

Brooks, P. (1984), *Reading for the Plot: Design and Intention in Narrative*. Oxford: Clarendon Press.

Brown, G. and G. Yule (1983), *Discourse Analysis*. Cambridge: Cambridge University Press.

Bruner, J. (1987), 'Life as Narrative', *Social Research*, 71: 691–710.

Bruner, J. (1991), 'The Narrative Construction of Reality', *Critical Inquiry*, 18 (1): 1–21.

Bruner, J. (2003), *Making Stories: Law, Literature, Life*. Cambridge, MA: Harvard University Press.

Bullitt, J. and W. J. Bate (1945), 'Distinctions between Fancy and Imagination in Eighteenth-Century English Criticism', *Modern Language Notes*, 60 (1): 8–15.

Burke, J. (2009), 'The Evil that Ordinary Men Can Do', *The Observer*, 22 February. Available online: http://www.theguardian.com/books/2009/feb/22/history-holocaust-books-jonathan-littell (accessed 20 August 2015).

Butler, A. C., N. A. Dennis and E. J. Marsh (2012), 'Inferring Facts from Fiction: Reading Correct and Incorrect Information Affects Memory for Related Information', *Memory*, 20 (5): 487–98.

Camerer, C. F., A. Dreber, F. Holzmeister, T.-H. Ho, J. Huber, M. Johannesson, M. Kirchler, G. Nave, B. A. Nosek, T. Pfeiffer, A. Altmejd, N. Buttrick, T. Chan, Y. Chen, E. Forsell, A. Gampa, E. Heikensten, L. Hummer, T. Imai, S. Isaksson, D. Manfredi, J. Rose, E.-J. Wagenmakers and H. Wu (2018), 'Evaluating the Replicability of Social Science Experiments in *Nature* and *Science* between 2010 and 2015', *Nature Human Behaviour*, 2: 637–44.

Camp, E. (2009), 'Two Varieties of Literary Imagination: Metaphor, Fiction, and Thought Experiments', *Midwest Studies in Philosophy: Poetry and Philosophy*, 33 (1): 107–30.

Caracciolo, M. and T. van Duuren (2015), 'Changed by Literature? A Critical Review of Psychological Research on the Effects of Reading Fiction', *Interdisciplinary Literary Studies*, 17 (4): 517–39.

Carr, D. (1985), 'Life and the Narrator's Art', in H. J. Silverman and D. Ihde (eds), *Hermeneutics and Deconstruction*, 108–21. Albany: SUNY Press.

Carroll, N. (1998), 'Art, Narrative, and Moral Understanding', in J. Levinson (ed.), *Aesthetics and Ethics: Essays at the Intersection*, 126–60. Cambridge: Cambridge University Press.

Carroll, N. (2002), 'The Wheel of Virtue: Art, Literature, and Moral Knowledge', *Journal of Aesthetics and Art Criticism*, 60 (1): 3–26.

Carroll, N. (2007a), 'Literary Realism, Recognition, and the Communication of Knowledge', in J. Gibson, W. Huemer and L. Pocci (eds), *A Sense of the World: Essays on Fiction, Narrative, and Knowledge*, 24–42. New York: Routledge.

Carroll, N. (2007b), 'Narrative Closure', *Philosophical Studies*, 135: 1–15.

Carroll, N. (2009), *On Criticism*. New York: Routledge.

Cave, T. (2014), 'Introduction', *Paragraph*, 37 (1): 1–14.

Cave, T. (2016), *Thinking with Literature: Towards a Cognitive Criticism*. Oxford: Oxford University Press.

Charlton, M., C. Pette and C. Burbaum (2004), 'Reading Strategies in Everyday Life: Different Ways of Reading a Novel Which Make a Distinction', *Poetics Today*, 25 (2): 241–63.

Chiaet, J., *Scientific American*, 4 October 2013, https://www.scientificamerican.com/article/novel-finding-reading-literary-fiction-improves-empathy/

Cohn, D. (1978), *Transparent Minds: Narrative Modes for Presenting Consciousness in Fiction*. Princeton: Princeton University Press.

Cohn, D. (1999), *The Distinction of Fiction*. Baltimore: Johns Hopkins University Press.

Coleridge, S. T. ([1817] 1983), *Biographia Literaria, or, Biographical Sketches of My Literary Life and Opinions Vol. I*. Princeton: Princeton University Press.

Connolly, J. W. (2013), *Dostoevsky's The Brothers Karamazov*. London: Bloomsbury.

Cooper, D. (1988), 'Life and Narrative', *International Journal of Moral and Social Studies*, 3: 161–72.

Cooper, N. (1995), 'The Epistemology of Understanding', *Inquiry: An Interdisciplinary Journal of Philosophy*, 38 (3): 205–15.

Crawford, M. (2009), *Shop Class as Soulcraft: An Inquiry into the Value of Work*. New York: Penguin Press.

Culler, J. (1975), *Structuralist Poetics: Structuralism, Linguistics, and the Study of Literature*. London: Routledge and Kegan Paul.

Culler, J. (1981), *The Pursuit of Signs: Semiotics, Literature, Deconstruction*. London: Routledge.

Currie, G. (1990), *The Nature of Fiction*. Cambridge: Cambridge University Press.

Currie, G. (2007), 'A Claim on the Reader', in I. Roth (ed.), *Imaginative Minds*, 169–86. Oxford: Oxford University Press.

Currie, G. (2010), *Narratives and Narrators: A Philosophy of Stories*. Oxford: Oxford University Press.

Currie, G. (2012), 'Literature and Truthfulness', in J. Maclaurin (ed.), *Rationis Defensor: Essays in Honour of Colin Cheyne*. Studies in History and Philosophy of Science, 28, 23–31. Dordrecht: Springer.

Currie, G. (2013), 'Does Great Literature Make Us Better?', *The New York Times*, 1 June. Available online: http://opinionator.blogs.nytimes.com/2013/06/01/does-great-literature-make-us-better/?_r=0 (accessed 6 June 2013).

Currie, G. (2014a), 'Standing in the Last Ditch: On the Communicative Intentions of Fiction Makers', *The Journal of Aesthetics and Art Criticism*, 72 (4): 351–63.

Currie, G. (2014b), 'On Getting Out of the Armchair to Do Aesthetics', in M. C. Haug (ed.), *Philosophical Methodology: The Armchair or the Laboratory?*, 435–50. New York: Routledge.

Currie, G. (2014c), 'Creativity and the Insight That Literature Brings', in E. S. Paul and S. B. Kaufman (eds), *The Philosophy of Creativity: New Essays*, 39–61. Oxford: Oxford University Press.

Currie, G. (2016a), 'Literature and "Theory of Mind"', in N. Carroll and J. Gibson (eds), *The Routledge Companion to Philosophy and Literature*, 419–29. New York: Routledge.

Currie, G. (2016b), 'Methods in the Philosophy of Literature and Film', in H. Cappelen, T. S. Gendler and J. Hawthorne (eds), *The Oxford Handbook of Philosophical Methodology*, 641–56. Oxford: Oxford University Press.

Currie, G. (2016c), 'Does Fiction Make Us Less Empathic?' *Teorema*, 35 (3): 47–68.

Danto, A. C. (1981), *The Transfiguration of the Commonplace*. Cambridge, MA: Harvard University Press.

Davis, C. (2013), 'Ethics, Stories and Reading', *SubStance*, 42 (2): 128–40.

Dennett, D. (1988), 'Why Everyone is a Novelist', *Times Literary Supplement*, September 16–22: 1028–9.

Derrida, J. (1972), 'La mythologie blanche. La métaphore dans le text philosophique', in Derrida, *Marges de la philosophie*, 247–324. Paris: Minuit.

Derrida, J. (1982), 'White Mythology: Metaphor in the Text of Philosophy' [La mythologie blanche. La métaphore dans le text philosophique], in Derrida, *Margins of Philosophy*, 207–71, trans. A. Bass. Brighton: The Harvester Press.

Djikic, M. and K. Oatley (2014), 'The Art in Fiction: From Indirect Communication to Self-Development', *Psychology of Aesthetics, Creativity, and the Arts*, 8 (4): 498–505.

Djikic, M., K. Oatley and M. Carland (2012), 'Genre or Artistic Merit: The Effect of Literature on Personality', *Scientific Study of Literature*, 2 (1): 25–36.

Djikic, M., K. Oatley and M. C. Moldoveanu (2013a), 'Reading Other Minds. Effects of Literature on Empathy', *Scientific Study of Literature*, 3 (1): 28–47.

Djikic, M., K. Oatley and M. C. Moldoveanu (2013b), 'Opening the Closed Mind: The Effect of Exposure to Literature on the Need for Closure', *Creativity Research Journal*, 25 (2): 149–54.

Djikic, M., K. Oatley, S. Zoeterman and J. B. Peterson (2009), 'On Being Moved by Art: How Reading Fiction Transforms the Self', *Creativity Research Journal*, 21 (1): 24–9.

Dodell-Feder, D. and D. I. Tamir (2018), 'Fiction Reading Has a Small Positive Impact on Social Cognition: A Meta-Analysis', *Journal of Experimental Psychology: General*, 147 (11): 1713–27.

Dorsch, F. (2012), *The Unity of Imagining*. Frankfurt: Ontos Verlag.

Eagleton, T. (2012), *The Event of Literature*. New Haven: Yale University Press.

Eakin, P. J. (1985), *Fictions in Autobiography*. Princeton: Princeton University Press.

Eakin, P. J. (1999), *How Our Lives Become Stories: Making Selves*. Ithaca: Cornell University Press.

Eakin, P. J. (2006), 'Narrative Identity and Narrative Imperialism: A Response to Galen Strawson and James Phelan', *Narrative*, 14 (2): 180–7.

Eco, U. ([1979] 1984), *The Role of the Reader: Explorations in the Semiotics of Texts*. Indianapolis: Indiana University Press.

Eco, U. (1989), *The Open Work* [Opera Aperta, 1962], trans. A. Cancogni. Cambridge, MA: Harvard University Press.

Eco, U. (1990), *The Limits of Interpretation*. Indianapolis: Indiana University Press.

Eco, U. ([1992] 2002), *Interpretation and Overinterpretation*, ed. S. Collini. Cambridge: Cambridge University Press.

Eco, U. (1994), *Six Walks in the Fictional Woods*. Cambridge, MA: Harvard University Press.

Eldridge, R. (2009), 'Introduction', in Eldridge (ed.), *The Oxford Handbook of Philosophy and Literature*, 3–15. Oxford: Oxford University Press.

Elgin, C. Z. ([1991] 1993), 'Understanding: Art and Science', *Synthese*, 95 (1): 13–28.

Elgin, C. Z. (1996), *Considered Judgment*. Princeton: Princeton University Press.

Elgin, C. Z. (2000), 'Reorienting Aesthetics, Reconceiving Cognition', *The Journal of Aesthetics and Art Criticism*, 58 (3): 219–25.

Elgin, C. Z. (2002), 'Art in the Advancement of Understanding', *American Philosophical Quarterly*, 39 (1): 1–12.

Elgin, C. Z. (2004), 'True Enough', *Philosophical Issues*, 14 (1): 113–31.

Elgin, C. Z. (2006), 'From Knowledge to Understanding', in S. Hetherington (ed.), *Epistemology Futures*, 199–215. Oxford: Clarendon Press.

Elgin, C. Z. (2007), 'Understanding and the Facts', *Philosophical Studies*, 132 (1): 33–42.

Elgin, C. Z. (2009), 'Is Understanding Factive?' in D. Pritchard, A. Miller and A. Haddock (eds), *Epistemic Value*, 322–30. Oxford: Oxford University Press.

Empson, W. (1965), *Seven Types of Ambiguity*. Third edition. Harmondsworth: Penguin Books.

Englund, P. (2011), *The Beauty and the Sorrow: An Intimate History of the First World War* [Stridens skönhet och sorg, 2008], trans. P. Graves. New York: Alfred A. Knopf.

Estess, T. L. (1974), 'The Inenarrable Contraption: Reflections on the Metaphor of Story', *Journal of the American Academy of Religion*, XLII (3): 415–34.

Feagin, S. (1997), *Reading with Feeling: The Aesthetics of Appreciation*. Ithaca: Cornell University Press.

Felski, R. (2008), *Uses of Literature*. Malden: Blackwell.

Fisher, W. (1987), *Human Communication as Narration: Toward a Philosophy of Reason, Value, and Action*. Columbia: University of South Carolina Press.

Fludernik, M. (1996), *Towards a 'Natural' Narratology*. New York: Routledge.

Fludernik, M. (2003), 'Natural Narratology and Cognitive Parameters', in D. Herman (ed.), *Narrative Theory and the Cognitive Sciences*, 243–67. Stanford: CSLI.

Fludernik, M. (2009), *An Introduction to Narratology*. New York: Routledge.

Fong, K., J. B. Mullin and R. A. Mar (2013), 'What You Read Matters: The Role of Fiction Genre in Predicting Interpersonal Sensitivity', *Psychology of Aesthetics, Creativity, and the Arts*, 7 (4): 370–6.

Foreman-Peck, L. (1983), 'Learning from Literature', *Journal of Aesthetic Education*, 17 (2): 57–69.

Freeman, M. (2017), 'Narrative at the Limits (Or: What Is "Life" Really Like?)', in B. Schiff, A. E. McKim and S. Patron (eds), *Life and Narrative: The Risks and Responsibilities of Storying Experience*, 11–27. Oxford: Oxford University Press.

French, P. A. (2001), *The Virtues of Vengeance*. Lawrence: University Press of Kansas.

Friend, S. (2008), 'Imagining Fact and Fiction', in K. Stock and K. Thomson-Jones (eds), *New Waves in Aesthetics*, 150–69. Basingstoke: Palgrave Macmillan.

Friend, S. (2011), 'Fictive Utterance and Imagining II', *Proceedings of the Aristotelian Society Suppl.*, 85: 163–80.

Friend, S. (2012), 'Fiction as Genre', *Proceedings of the Aristotelian Society*, 112 (2): 179–209.

Friend, S. (2014), 'Believing in Stories', in G. Currie, Matthew Kieran, Aaron Meskin and Jon Robson (eds), *Aesthetics and the Sciences of Mind*, 227–47. Oxford: Oxford University Press.

Gallagher, S. (2015), 'Why We Are Not All Novelists', in P. F. Bundgaard and F. Stjernfelt (eds), *Investigations into the Phenomenology and the Ontology of the Work of Art: What Are Artworks and How Do We Experience Them?*, 129–43. London: SpringerOpen.

Gang, J. (2013), 'Mindless Modernism', *Novel*, 46 (1): 116–32.

Gaskin, R. (2013), *Language, Truth, and Literature: A Defense of Literary Humanism*. Oxford: Oxford University Press.

Gaut, B. (2007), *Art, Emotion and Ethics*. Oxford: Oxford University Press.

Gerrig, R. J. (1991), *Experiencing Narrative Worlds: On the Psychological Activities of Reading*. New Haven: Westview Press.

Gerrig, R. J. and D. A. Prentice (1991), 'The Representation of Fictional Information', *Psychological Science*, 2 (5): 336–40.

Gerrig, R. J. and D. N. Rapp (2004), 'Psychological Processes Underlying Literary Impact', *Poetics Today*, 25 (2): 265–81.

Gerrig, R. J. and G. Egidi (2003), 'Cognitive Psychological Foundations of Narrative Experiences', in David Herman (ed.), *Narrative Theory and the Cognitive Sciences*, 33–55. Stanford: CSLI Publications.

Gibson, J. (2004), 'Reading for Life', in J. Gibson and W. Huemer (eds), *The Literary Wittgenstein*, 109–24. London: Routledge.

Gibson, J. (2007), *Fiction and the Weave of Life*. Oxford: Oxford University Press.

Gibson, J. (2008), 'Cognitivism and the Arts', *Philosophy Compass*, 3 (4): 573–89.

Glover, J. (1988), *I: The Philosophy and Psychology of Personal Identity*. London: Penguin.

Goldie, P. (2012), *The Mess Inside. Narrative, Emotion, and the Mind*. Oxford: Oxford University Press.

Goldman, A. H. (2013), *Philosophy and the Novel*. Oxford: Oxford University Press.

Goodman, N. (1978), *Ways of Worldmaking*. Indianapolis: Hackett Publishing.

Goodman, N. and C. Z. Elgin (1988), *Reconceptions in Philosophy and Other Arts and Sciences*. London: Routledge.

Graesser, A., B. Olde and B. Klettke (2002), 'How Does the Mind Construct and Represent Stories?', in M. C. Green, J. J. Strange and T. C. Brock (eds), *Narrative Impact: Social and Cognitive Foundations*, 229–62. Mahwah: Erlbaum.

Graham, G. ([1997] 2000), *Philosophy of the Arts: An Introduction to Aesthetics*. Second edition. London: Routledge.

Green, M. C. and T. C. Brock (2000), 'The Role of Transportation in the Persuasiveness of Public Narratives', *Journal of Personality and Social Psychology*, 79 (5): 701–21.

Green, M. C. and T. C. Brock (2002), 'In the Mind's Eye: Transportation-Imagery Model of Mental Persuasion', in M. C. Green, J. J. Strange and T. C. Brock (eds), *Narrative Impact. Social and Cognitive Foundations*, 315–41. Mahwah: Erlbaum.

Greene, T. M. (1938), 'Beauty and the Cognitive Significance of Art', *The Journal of Philosophy*, 35 (14): 365–81.

Greene, T. M. (1940), *The Arts and the Art of Criticism*. Princeton: Princeton University Press.

Greenfieldboyce, Nell, NPR, 4 October 2013, https://www.npr.org/sections/health-shots/2013/10/04/229190837/want-to-read-others-thoughts-try-reading-literary-fiction?t=1571657876705

Grimm, S. R. (2012), 'The Value of Understanding', *Philosophy Compass*, 7 (2): 103–17.

Grimm, S. R., C. Baumberger and S. Ammon, eds (2016), *Explaining Understanding: New Perspectives from Epistemology and Philosophy of Science*. New York: Routledge.

Gros, F. (2015), *A Philosophy of Walking* [Marcher, une philosophie, 2008], trans. J. Howe. London: Verso.

Haaparanta, L. (2019), 'On Knowing the Other's Emotions', in F. Kjosavik, C. Beyer and C. Fricke (eds), *Husserl's Phenomenology of Intersubjectivity: Historical Interpretations and Contemporary Applications*, 165–77. New York: Routledge.

Haden, J., *Inc.*, 19 November 2015, https://www.inc.com/jeff-haden/9-ways-reading-fiction-can-make-you-happier-and-more-creative.html

Hagberg, G. (1994), *Meaning and Interpretation: Wittgenstein, Henry James, and Literary Knowledge*. Ithaca: Cornell University Press.

Hakemulder, F., O. Fialho and P. M. Bal (2016), 'Learning from Literature. Empirical Research on Readers in Schools and at the Workplace', in M. Burke, O. Fialho and S. Zyngier (eds), *Scientific Approaches to Literature in Learning Environments*, 19–38. Amsterdam: John Benjamins Publishing Company.

Hakemulder, J. [Frank] (2000), *The Moral Laboratory: Experiments Examining the Effects of Reading Literature on Social Perception and Moral Self-Concept*. Amsterdam: John Benjamins Publishing Company.

Hamburger, K. ([1957] 1968), *Die Logik der Dichtung*. Stuttgart: Ernst Klett Verlag.

Hamburger, K. ([1973] 1993), *The Logic of Literature* [Die Logik der Dichtung, 1957]. Bloomington: Indiana University Press.

Hardy, B. (1968), 'Towards a Poetics of Fiction: An Approach through Narrative', *NOVEL: A Forum of Fiction*, 2 (1): 5–14.

Harold, J. (2016), 'Literary Cognitivism', in N. Carroll and J. Gibson (eds), *The Routledge Companion to Philosophy of Literature*, 382–93. New York: Routledge.

Harrison, B. (1991), *Inconvenient Fictions. Literature and the Limits of Theory*. New Haven: Yale University Press.

Harrison, B. (2015), *What Is Fiction For? Literary Humanism Restored*. Bloomington: Indiana University Press.

Heider, F. and M. Simmel (1944), 'An Experimental Study of Apparent Behavior', *American Journal of Psychology*, 57 (2): 243–59.

Hempfer, K. W. (2004), 'Some Problems Concerning a Theory of Fiction(ality)', *Style*, 38 (3): 302–24.

Herman, D. (2007), 'Introduction', in D. Herman (ed.), *The Cambridge Companion to Narrative*, 3–21. Cambridge: Cambridge University Press.

Herman, D. (2011), '1880–1945 Re-minding Modernism', in Herman (ed.), *The Emergence of Mind. Representations of Consciousness in Narrative Discourse in English*, 243–72. Lincoln: University of Nebraska Press.

Hintikka, J. (1979), 'Virginia Woolf and Our Knowledge of the External World', *The Journal of Aesthetics and Art Criticism*, 38 (1): 5–14.

Huemer, W. (2019), 'Power and Limits of a Picture: On the Notion of Thought Experiments in Philosophy of Literature', in F. Bornmüller, M. Lessau and J. Franzen (eds), *Literature as Thought Experiment?* 71–82. Paderborn: Fink.

Hutto, D. D. (2007a), 'Narrative and Understanding Persons', in Hutto (ed.), *Narrative and Understanding Persons*, 1–15. Cambridge: Cambridge University Press.

Hutto, D. D. (2007b), 'Narrative Practice Hypothesis: Origins and Applications of Folk Psychology', in D. D. Hutto (ed.), *Narrative and Understanding Persons*, 43–68. Cambridge: Cambridge University Press.

Hyvärinen, M. (2012), '"Against Narrativity" Reconsidered', in G. Rossholm and C. Johansson (eds), *Disputable Core Concepts of Narrative Theory*, 327–45. Bern: Peter Lang.

Hyvärinen, M., Lars-Christer Hydén, Marja Saarenheimo and Maria Tamboukou, eds (2010), *Beyond Narrative Coherence: An Introduction*. Philadelphia: John Benjamins Pub. Company.

Ichino, A. and G. Currie (2016), 'Truth and Trust in Fiction', in E. Sullivan-Bissett, H. Bradley and P. Noordhof (eds), *Art and the Nature of Belief*, 63–82. Oxford: Oxford University Press.

Ingarden, R. ([1973] 1979), *The Cognition of the Literary Work of Art* [Vom Erkennen des literarischen Kunstwerks, 1968], trans. R. A. Crowley and K. R. Olson. Evanston: Northwestern University Press.

Isenberg, A. (1987/1950), 'Analytical Philosophy and the Study of Art', *Journal of Aesthetics and Art Criticism*, 46 (3): 125–36.

Iser, W. (1971), 'Indeterminacy and the Reader's Response in Prose Fiction', in J. Hillis Miller (ed.), *Aspects of Narrative*, 1–45. New York: Columbia University Press.

Iser, W. (1972), 'The Reading Process: A Phenomenological Approach', *New Literary History*, 3 (2): 279–99.

Iser, W. ([1974] 1978), *The Implied Reader: Patterns of Communication in Prose Fiction from Bunyan to Beckett* [Der implizite Leser: Kommunikationsformen des Romans von Bunyan bis Beckett, 1972]. Baltimore: The Johns Hopkins University Press.

Iser, W. ([1978] 1987), *The Act of Reading: A Theory of Aesthetic Response* [Der Akt des Lesens. Theorie ästhetischer Wirkung, 1976]. Baltimore: The Johns Hopkins University Press.

John, E. (1998), 'Reading Fiction and Conceptual Knowledge: Philosophical Thought in Literary Context', *Journal of Aesthetics and Art Criticism*, 56 (4): 331–48.

Johnson, D. R. (2012), 'Transportation into a Story Increases Empathy, Prosocial Behavior, and Perceptual Bias toward Fearful Expressions', *Personality and Individual Differences*, 52 (2): 150–5.

Johnson, D. R., G. K. Cushman, L. A. Borden and M. S. McCune (2013), 'Potentiating Empathic Growth: Generating Imagery while Reading Fiction Increases Empathy and Prosocial Behavior', *Psychology of Aesthetics, Creativity, and the Arts*, 7 (3): 306–12.

Jones, M. V. (1992), Introduction to *Brothers Karamazov*. New York: Knopf.

Kearney, R. (1988), *The Wake of Imagination. Toward a Postmodern Culture*. London: Routledge.

Keen, S. (2007), *Empathy and the Novel*. Oxford: Oxford University Press.

Kerby, A. P. (1991), *Narrative and the Self*. Bloomington: Indiana University Press.

Kermode, F. ([1967] 2000), *The Sense of an Ending: Studies in the Theory of Fiction*. Oxford: Oxford University Press.

Kidd, D. C. and E. Castano (2013a), 'Reading Literary Fiction Improves Theory of Mind', *Science*, 342 (6156): 377–80.

Kidd, D. C. and E. Castano (2013b), Supplementary Materials for 'Reading Literary Fiction Improves Theory of Mind', Science Express, 3 October 2013. Revised 4 October 2013. Internet: www.sciencemag.org/cgi/content/full/science.1239918/DC1

Kidd, D. C. and E. Castano (2017), 'Panero et al. (2016): Failure to Replicate Methods Caused the Failure to Replicate Results', *Journal of Personality and Social Psychology*, 112 (3): e1–4.

Kidd, D. and E. Castano (2018a), 'Reading Literary Fiction and Theory of Mind: Three Preregistered Replications and Extensions of Kidd and Castano (2013)', *Social Psychological and Personality Science*, 10 (4): 522–31.

Kidd, D. and E. Castano (2018b), 'Reading Literary Fiction Can Improve Theory of Mind', *Nature Human Behaviour*, 2: 604.

Kidd, D., M. Ongis and E. Castano (2016), 'On Literary Fiction and Its Effects on Theory of Mind', *Scientific Study of Literature*, 6 (1): 42–58.

Kivy, P. (1995), *Philosophies of Arts: An Essay in Differences*. Cambridge: Cambridge University Press.

Kivy, P. (1997), 'On the Banality of Literary Truths', *Philosophic Exchange*, 28: 17–27.

Kivy, P. (2006), *The Performance of Reading*. Malden: Blackwell.

Kivy, P. (2011), *Once-Told Tales*. Malden: Blackwell.

Koopman, E. M. (2015), 'Empathic Reactions After Reading: The Role of Genre, Personal Factors and Affective Responses', *Poetics*, 50: 62–79.

Koopman, E. M. and F. Hakemulder (2015), 'Effects of Literature on Empathy and Self- Reflection: A Theoretical-Empirical Framework', *Journal of Literary Theory*, 9 (1): 79–111.

Kornblith, H. ([2012] 2014), *On Reflection*. Oxford: Oxford University Press.

Kreiswirth, M. (2000), 'Merely Telling Stories? Narrative and Knowledge in the Human Sciences', *Poetics Today*, 21 (2): 293–318.

van Kuijk, I., Peter Verkoeijen, Katinka Dijkstra and Rolf A. Zwaan (2018), 'The Effect of Reading a Short Passage of Literary Fiction on Theory of Mind: A Replication of Kidd and Castano (2013)', *Collabra: Psychology*, 4 (1): 1–7.

Kuiken, D., D. S. Miall and S. Sikora (2004), 'Forms of Self-Implication in Literary Reading', *Poetics Today*, 25 (2): 171–203.

Kundera, M. ([1988] 1999), *The Art of the Novel* [*L'Art du roman*, 1986], trans. L. Asher. New York: Faber and Faber.

Kvanvig, J. L. (2003), *The Value of Knowledge and the Pursuit of Understanding*. Cambridge: Cambridge University Press.

Kvanvig, J. L. (2011), 'Millar on the Value of Knowledge', *Aristotelian Society Supplementary*, 85: 83–99.

Lamarque, P. (1997), 'Learning from Literature', *The Dalhousie Review*, 77 (1): 7–21.

Lamarque, P. (2009), *The Philosophy of Literature*. Malden: Blackwell.

Lamarque, P. (2010a), 'The Uselessness of Art', *The Journal of Aesthetics and Art Criticism*, 68 (3): 205–14.

Lamarque, P. (2010b), 'Literature and Truth', in G. Hagberg and W. Jost (eds), *Companion to the Philosophy of Literature*, 367–84. New York: Wiley-Blackwell.

Lamarque, P. (2012), 'Thought Theory and Literary Cognition', in J. Daiber, Eva-Maria Konrad and Thomas Petraschka (eds), *Understanding Fiction: Knowledge and Meaning in Literature*, 67–80. Münster: Mentis.

Lamarque, P. (2014), *The Opacity of Narrative*. London: Rowman and Littlefield International.

Lamarque, P. (2016), 'Belief, Thought, and Literature', in E. Sullivan-Bissett, H. Bradley and P. Noordhof (eds), *Art and Belief*, 100–18. Oxford: Oxford University Press.

Lamarque, P. (2019), 'Narrative and Emotion: On Not Getting Too Carried Away', *Instrumental Narratives blog*, 10 December. Available online: https ://instrumentalnarratives.wordpress.com/2019/12/10/peter-lamarque -narrative-and-emotion-on-not-getting-too-carried-away/ (accessed 10 December 2019).

Lamarque, P. and S. H. Olsen (1994), *Truth, Fiction, and Literature. A Philosophical Perspective*. Oxford: Clarendon Press.

Landy, J. (2012), *How to Do Things with Fictions*. Oxford: Oxford University Press.

Van Leeuwen, N. (2011), 'Imagination Is Where the Action Is', *Journal of Philosophy*, 108 (2): 55–77.

Levi, P. (1989), *The Drowned and the Saved* [I sommersi e i salvati, 1986], trans. R. Rosenthal. New York: Penguin.

Levinson, J. (1997), 'Review of Truth, Fiction, and Literature: A Philosophical Perspective, by Peter Lamarque and Stein Haugom Olsen', *Philosophy and Phenomenological Research*, 57 (4): 964–8.

Livingston, P. (2009), 'Narrativity and Knowledge', in N. Carroll (ed.), *The Poetics, Aesthetics, and Philosophy of Narrative*, 25–36. Malden: Blackwell.

Löschnigg, M. (2010), 'Postclassical Narratology and the Theory of Autobiography', in J. Alber and M. Fludernik (eds), *Postclassical Narratology: Approaches and Analyses*, 255–74. Columbus: Ohio State University Press.

Lukits, A., *The Wall Street Journal*, 7 March 2016, https://www.wsj.com/artic les/reading-fiction-may-enhance-social-skills-1457366832

MacIntyre, A. ([1981] 2007), *After Virtue. A Study in Moral Theory*. Notre Dame: University of Notre Dame Press.

Mäkelä, M. (2013), 'Cycles of Narrative Necessity: Suspect Tellers and the Textuality of Fictional Minds', in L. Bernaerts, Dirk De Geest, Luc Herman and Bart Vervaeck (eds), *Stories and Minds: Cognitive Approaches to Literary Narrative*, 129–51. Lincoln: University of Nebraska Press.

Malcolm, N. ([1958] 2001), *Ludwig Wittgenstein: A Memoir*. Oxford: Clarendon Press.

Mar, R. A. (2018a), 'Stories and the Promotion of Social Cognition', *Current Directions in Psychological Science*, 27 (4): 1–6.

Mar, R. A. (2018b), 'Evaluating Whether Stories Can Promote Social Cognition: Introducing the Social Processes and Content Entrained by Narrative (SPaCEN) Framework', *Discourse Processes*, 55 (5–6): 454–79.

Mar, R. A., J. Peskin and K. Fong (2010), 'Literary Arts and the Development of the Life Story', *New Directions for Child and Adolescent Development*, 131: 73–84.

Mar, R. A. and K. Oatley (2008), 'The Function of Fiction is the Abstraction and Simulation of Social Experience', *Perspectives on Psychological Science*, 3 (3): 173–92.

Mar, R. A., K. Oatley, J. Hirsh, J. dela Paz and J. B. Peterson (2006), 'Bookworms versus Nerds: Exposure to Fiction versus Non-Fiction, Divergent Associations with Social Ability, and the Simulation of Fictional Social Worlds', *Journal of Research in Personality*, 40 (5): 694–712.

Mar, R. A., K. Oatley and J. B. Peterson (2009), 'Exploring the Link between Reading Fiction and Empathy: Ruling Out Individual Differences and Examining Outcomes', *Communications*, 34 (4): 407–28.

Marsh, E. J. and L. Fazio (2006), 'Learning Errors from Fiction: Difficulties in Reducing Reliance on Fictional Stories', *Memory and Cognition*, 34 (4): 1140–9.

Marsh, E. J., M. L. Meade and H. L. Roediger III (2003), 'Learning Facts from Fiction', *Journal of Memory and Language*, 49: 519–36.

Martin, T. (2009), 'The Danger for Mankind Is Me and You', *The Telegraph*, 05 March 2009. Internet: www.telegraph.co.uk/culture/books/bookreviews/4942961/The-danger-for-mankind-is-me-and-you.html (cited 20 August 2015).

Martindale, C. (1996), 'Empirical Questions Deserve Empirical Answers', *Philosophy and Literature*, 20 (2): 347–61.

Matravers, D. ([1998] 2001), *Art and Emotion*. Oxford: Clarendon Press.

Matravers, D. (2014), *Fiction and Narrative*. Oxford: Oxford University Press.

Matravers, D. (2018), 'Recent Philosophy and the Fiction/Non-fiction Distinction', *Collection and Curation*, 37 (2): 93–6. Available online: http://dx.doi.org/doi:10.1108/cc-07-2017-0031 (accessed 3 April 2018).

Matz, J. (2006), 'The Novel', in D. Bradshaw and K. J. H. Dettmar (eds), *A Companion to Modernist Literature and Culture*, 215–26. Malden: Blackwell.

McHale, B. (1987), *Postmodernist Fiction*. London: Methuen.

Mehtonen, P. (2003), *Obscure Language, Unclear Literature: Theory and Practice from Quintilian to the Enlightenment*, trans. R. MacGilleon. Helsinki: The Finnish Academy of Science and Letters.

Meisel, P. (2007), *The Literary Freud*. London: Routledge.

Miall, D. S. (2000), 'On the Necessity of Empirical Studies of Literary Reading', *Frame. Utrecht Journal of Literary Theory*, 14 (2–3): 43–59.

Miall, D. S. (2005), 'Beyond Interpretation: The Cognitive Significance of Reading', in H. Veivo, B. Pettersson and M. Polvinen (eds), *Cognition and Literary Interpretation in Practice*, 129–56. Helsinki: University of Helsinki Press.

Miall, D. S. (2006), 'Empirical Approaches to Studying Literary Readers: The State of the Discipline', *Book History*, 9: 291–311.

Miall, D. S. (2008), 'Resisting Interpretation', in N. Dunn (ed.), *Tarkovsky*, 320–33. London: Black Dog Publishing.

Miall, D. S. and D. Kuiken (1994), 'Foregrounding, Defamiliarization, and Affect: Response to Literary Stories', *Poetics*, 22 (5): 389–407.

Miall, D. S. and D. Kuiken (1999), 'What Is Literariness? Three Components of Literary Reading', *Discourse Processes*, 28 (2): 121–38.

Miesen, H. W. J. M. (2003), 'Predicting and Explaining Literary Reading: An Application of the Theory of Planned Behavior', *Poetics*, 31 (3–4): 189–212.

Mikkonen, J. (2013), *The Cognitive Value of Philosophical Fiction*. London: Bloomsbury.

Mill, J. S. ([1873] 2009), *Autobiography of J. S. Mill*. New York: Cosimo Classics.

Miller, R. F. (2008), *The Brothers Karamazov: Worlds of the Novel*. New Haven: Yale University Press.

Mink, L. O. ([1978] 2001), 'Narrative Form as a Cognitive Instrument', in G. Roberts (ed.), *The History and Narrative Reader*, 211–20. London: Routledge.

Mothersill, M. (1984), *Beauty Restored*. Oxford: Clarendon Press.

Murdoch, I. (1993), *Metaphysics as a Guide to Morals*. London: Penguin.

Nair, R. B. (2003), *Narrative Gravity: Conversation, Cognition, Culture*. London: Routledge.

Novitz, D. (1987), *Knowledge, Fiction, and Imagination*. Philadelphia: Temple University Press.

Novitz, D. ([1992] 2001), *The Boundaries of Art: A Philosophical Inquiry into the Place of Art in Everyday Life*. Christchurch: Cybereditions.

Novitz, D. (2004), 'Knowledge and Art', in I. Niiniluoto, M. Sintonen and J. Wolenski (eds), *Handbook of Epistemology*, 985–1012. Dordrect: Kluwer.

Nussbaum, M. (1990), *Love's Knowledge: Essays on Philosophy and Literature*. New York: Oxford University Press.

Oatley, K. (1994), 'A Taxonomy of the Emotions of Literary Response and a Theory of Identification in Fictional Narrative', *Poetics*, 23 (1–2): 53–74.

Oatley, K. (1999), 'Why Fiction May Be Twice as True as Fact: Fiction as Cognitive and Emotional Simulation', *Review of General Psychology*, 3 (2): 101–17.

Oatley, K. (2011), *Such Stuff as Dreams: The Psychology of Fiction*. Oxford: Wiley-Blackwell.

Oatley, K. (2016), 'Fiction: Simulation of Social Worlds', *Trends in Cognitive Sciences*, 20 (8): 618–28.

Olsen, S. H. (1987), *The End of Literary Theory*. Cambridge: University Press.

Palmer, A. (2004), *Fictional Minds*. Lincoln: University of Nebraska Press.

Palmer, A. (2010), *Social Minds in the Novel*. Columbus: Ohio State University Press.

Palmer, A. (2011), '1945– Ontologies of Consciousness', in D. Herman (ed.), *The Emergence of Mind. Representations of Consciousness in Narrative Discourse in English*, 273–97. Lincoln: University of Nebraska Press.

Panero, M. E., D. S. Weisberg, J. Black, T. R. Goldstein, J. L. Barnes, H. Brownell and E. Winner (2016), 'Does Reading a Single Passage of Literary Fiction Really Improve Theory of Mind? An Attempt at Replication', *Journal of Personality and Social Psychology*, 111 (5): e46–e54.

Panero, M. E., D. S. Weisberg, J. Black, T. R. Goldstein, J. L. Barnes, H. Brownell and E. Winner (2017), 'No Support for the Claim That Literary Fiction Uniquely and Immediately Improves Theory of Mind: A Reply to Kidd and Castano's Commentary on Panero et al. (2016)', *Journal of Personality and Social Psychology*, 112 (3): e5–8.

Pascal, R. (1960), *Design and Truth in Autobiography*. London: Routledge and Kegan Paul.

Paul, A. M., *Time*, 3 June 2013, http://ideas.time.com/2013/06/03/why-we-should-read-literature/

Pettersson, A. (2011), 'Literary Studies and Human Priorities', in S. H. Olsen and A. Pettersson (eds), *Why Literary Studies?* 29–59. Oslo: Novus Forlag.

Pettersson, A. (2012), *The Concept of Literary Application: Readers' Analogies from Text to Life*. New York: Palgrave Macmillan.

Pettersson, B. (2016), *How Literary Worlds Are Shaped: A Comparative Poetics of Literary Imagination*. Berlin: De Gruyter.

Pettersson, T. (2002), 'The Literary Work as a Pliable Entity: Combining Realism and Pluralism', in M. Krausz (ed.), *Is There a Single Right Interpretation?*, 211–30. University Park: The Pennsylvania State University Press.

Phelan, J. (2005), 'Editor's Column: Who's Here? Thoughts on Narrative Identity and Narrative Imperialism', *Narrative*, 13 (3): 205–10.

Phillips, D. Z. ([1972] 1982), 'Allegiance and Change in Morality: A Study in Contrasts', in Phillips, *Through a Darkening Glass: Philosophy, Literature, and Cultural Change*, 9–29. Oxford: Basil Blackwell.

Pillow, K. (2009), 'Imagination', in R. Eldridge (ed.), *The Oxford Handbook of Philosophy and Literature*, 349–68. Oxford: Oxford University Press.

Pino, M. C. and M. Mazza (2016), 'The Use of "Literary Fiction" to Promote Mentalizing Ability', *PLoS One*, 11 (8): e0160254.

Polkinghorne, D. E. (1991), 'Narrative and Self-Concept', *Journal of Narrative and Life History*, 1 (2–3): 135–53.

Polkinghorne, D. E. ([1995] 2003), 'Narrative Configuration in Qualitative Analysis', in J. A. Hatch and R. Wisniewski (eds), *Life, History and Narrative*, 5–24. London: The Falmer Press.

Polvinen, M. (2017), 'Cognitive Science and the Double Vision of Fiction', in M. Burke and E. T. Troscianko (eds), *Cognitive Literary Science: Dialogues between Literature and Cognition*, 135–50. Oxford: Oxford University Press.

Posner, R. (1997), 'Against Ethical Criticism', *Philosophy and Literature*, 21 (1): 1–27.

Posner, R. (1998), 'Against Ethical Criticism: Part Two', *Philosophy and Literature*, 22 (2): 394–412.

Pouivet, R. (2011), 'Modal Aesthetics', *Proceedings of the European Society for Aesthetics*, 3: 15–27. Available online: http://proceedings.eurosa.org/3/pouivet2011.pdf

Poulet, G. (1969), 'Phenomenology of Reading', *New Literary History*, 1 (1): 53–68.

Prado, C. G. (1984), *Making Believe*. Westport: Greenwood Press.

Prentice, D. A., R. J. Gerrig and D. S. Bailis (1997), 'What Readers Bring to the Processing of Fictional Texts', *Psychonomic Bulletin and Review*, 4 (3): 416–20.

Prentice, D. A. and R. J. Gerrig (1999), 'Exploring the Boundary between Fiction and Reality', in S. Chaiken and Y. Trope (eds), *Dual-Process Theories in Social Psychology*, 529–46. New York: Guilford Press.

Putnam, H. (1978), *Meaning and the Moral Sciences*. London: Routledge and Kegan Paul.

Putnam, H. (1979), 'Reflections on Goodman's *Ways of Worldmaking*', *The Journal of Philosophy*, 76 (11): 603–18.

Quigley, M. M. (2008), 'Modern Novel and Vagueness', *Modernism/modernity*, 15 (1): 101–29.

Randall, W. L. (2014), *The Stories We Are: An Essay on Self-Creation*. Second edition. Toronto: University of Toronto Press.

Reid, L. A. (1969), *Meaning in the Arts*. London: George Allen & Unwin Ltd.

Richardson, S. ([1740] 1825), *Pamela; or, Virtue Rewarded*. London: J. M'Gowan.

Richell, R. A., D. G. V. Mitchell, C. Newman, A. Leonard, S. Baron-Cohen and R. J. R. Blair (2003), 'Theory of Mind and Psychopathy: Can Psychopathic Individuals Read the "Language of the Eyes"?', *Neuropsychologia*, 41 (5): 523–6.

Ricœur, P. (1985), 'History as Narrative and Practice', *Philosophy Today*, 29 (3–4): 213–22.

Ricœur, P. (1990), *Time and Narrative I* [Temps et récit, 1983], trans. K. McLaughlin and D. Pellauer. Chicago: The University of Chicago Press.

Ricœur, P. (1992), *Oneself as Another* [Soi-même comme un autre, 1990], trans. K. Blamey. Chicago: University of Chicago Press.

Robinson, J. (2005), *Deeper Than Reason: Emotion and Its Role in Literature, Music, and Art*. Oxford: Oxford University Press.

Rose, J. (1992), 'Rereading the English Common Reader: A Preface to a History of Audiences', *Journal of the History of Ideas*, 53: 47–70.

Ross, S. (2012), 'Comparing and Sharing Taste: Reflections on Critical Advice', *Journal of Aesthetics and Art Criticism*, 70 (4): 363–71.

Rowe, M. (1997), 'Lamarque and Olsen on Literature and Truth', *Philosophical Quarterly*, 47 (188): 322–41.

Ryan, M.-L. (1991), *Possible World, Artificial Intelligence, and Narrative Theory*. Bloomington: Indiana University Press.

Ryan, M.-L. (2007), 'Toward a Definition of Narrative', in D. Herman (ed.), *The Cambridge Companion to Narrative*, 22–36. Cambridge: Cambridge University Press.

Samur, D., M. Tops and S. L. Koole (2018), 'Does a Single Session of Reading Literary Fiction Prime Enhanced Mentalising Performance? Four Replication Experiments of Kidd and Castano (2013)', *Cognition and Emotion*, 32 (1): 130–44.

Sartre, J.-P. (1943), *L'Être et le Néant*. Paris: Gallimard.

Sartwell, C. (2000), *End of Story: Toward an Annihilation of Language and History*. Albany: SUNY Press.

Schechtman, M. (2011), 'The Narrative Self', in S. Gallagher (ed.), *The Oxford Handbook of the Self*, 413–15. Oxford: Oxford University Press.

Schechtman, M. (2016), 'A Mess Indeed: Empathic Access, Narrative, and Identity', in J. Dodd (ed.), *Art, Mind, and Narrative: Themes from the Work of Peter Goldie*, 17–34. Oxford: Oxford University Press.

Schonfeld, Z., *The Atlantic*, 4 October 2013, https://www.theatlantic.com/entertainment/archive/2013/10/now-we-have-proof-reading-literary-fiction-makes-you-better-person/309996/

Schopenhauer, A. ([1958] 1966), *The World as Will and Representation Vol. II*. [*Die Welt als Wille und Vorstellung*, 1918 and 1844], trans. E. F. J. Payne. New York: Dover Press.

Schopenhauer, A. (1974), *Parerga and Paralipomena. Short Philosophical Essays. Vol. II* [Parerga und Paralipomena: kleine philosophische Schriften, 1851], trans. E. F. J. Payne. Oxford: Clarendon Press.

Searle, J. R. (1975), 'The Logical Status of Fictional Discourse', *New Literary History*, 6 (2): 319–32.

Shils, E. (1981), *Tradition*. London: Faber and Faber.

Shusterman, R. (1989), 'Introduction: Analysing Analytic Aesthetics', in Shusterman (ed.), *Analytic Aesthetics*, 1–19. Oxford: Blackwell.

Stace, W. T. and T. M. Greene (1938), 'Comments and Criticisms', *The Journal of Philosophy*, 35 (24): 656–8.

Stanford, W. B. ([1939] 1972), *Ambiguity in Greek Literature. Studies in Theory and Practice*. New York: Johnson Reprint Corp.

Stecker, R. (2003), 'The Aesthetic Experience of Literature and Its Cognitive Value', in A. Sukla (ed.), *Art and Experience*, 91–108. Westport: Praeger.

Stock, K. (2014), 'Physiological Evidence and the Paradox of Fiction', in G. Currie et al. (eds), *Aesthetics and the Sciences of Mind*, 205–26. Oxford: Oxford University Press.

Stock, K. and K. Thomson-Jones (2008), 'Introduction', to Stock and Thomson-Jones (eds), *New Waves in Aesthetics*, xi–xix. Houndmills: Palgrave-Macmillan.

Stolnitz, J. (1992), 'On the Cognitive Triviality of Art', *British Journal of Aesthetics*, 32 (3): 191–200.

Strawson, G. (2004), 'Against Narrativity', *Ratio*, 17 (4): 428–52.

Tamir, D. I., Andrew B. Bricker, David Dodell-Feder and Jason P. Mitchell (2016), 'Reading Fiction and Reading Minds: The Role of Simulation in the Default Network', *Social Cognitive and Affective Neuroscience*, 11 (2): 215–24.

Taylor, C. (1989), *Sources of the Self: The Making of the Modern Identity*. Cambridge, MA: Harvard University Press.

Toolan, M. (2009), 'Coherence', in P. Hühn (ed.), *Handbook of Narratology*, 44–62. Berlin: de Gruyter.

Toolan, M. ([2011] 2013), 'Coherence', in P. Hühn, J. Pier, W. Schmid and J. Schönert (eds), *The Living Handbook of Narratology*. Created 29. September 2011, revised 1 October 2013. Hamburg: Hamburg University. Available online: http://www.lhn.uni-hamburg.de/article/coherence (accessed 1 October 2013).

Trombetta, S., *Bustle*, 31 October 2017, https://www.bustle.com/p/why-readers-are-generally-more-thoughtful-people-according-to-science-3067173

Turner, M. (1996), *The Literary Mind*. Oxford: Oxford University Press.

Velleman, D. J. (2003), 'Narrative Explanation', *The Philosophical Review*, 112 (1): 1–25.

Velleman, D. J. (2005), 'The Self as Narrator', in J. Christman and J. Anderson (eds), *Autonomy and the Challenges to Liberalism: New* Essays, 56–76. Cambridge: Cambridge University Press.

Walsh, D. (1943), 'The Cognitive Content of Art', *Philosophical Review*, 52 (5): 433–51.

Walton, K. L. (1978), 'How Remote Are Fictional Worlds from the Real World?' *Journal of Aesthetics and Art Criticism*, 37 (1): 11–23.

Walton, K. L. (1990), *Mimesis as Make-Believe: On the Foundations of the Representational Arts*. Cambridge, MA: Harvard University Press.

Wheeler, C., M. C. Green and T. C. Brock (1999), 'Fictional Narratives Change Beliefs: Replications of Prentice, Gerrig, and Bailis (1997) with Mixed Corroboration', *Psychonomic Bulletin and Review*, 6 (1): 136–41.

White, A. (1981), *The Uses of Obscurity: The Fiction of Early Modernism*. London: Routledge and Kegan Paul.

Whiteman, H., *Medical News Today*, 12 October 2016, https://www.medicalnewstoday.com/articles/313429.php

Willems, R. M. and A. M. Jacobs (2016), 'Caring About Dostoyevsky: The Untapped Potential of Studying Literature', *Trends in Cognitive Sciences*, 20 (4): 243–5.

Williams, B. (2009), 'Life as Narrative', *European Journal of Philosophy*, 17 (2): 305–14.

Wilson, C. ([1983] 2004), 'Literature and Knowledge', in E. John and D. M. Lopes (eds), *Philosophy of Literature: Contemporary and Classic Readings*, 324–8. Oxford: Blackwell.
Winch, P. (1972), *Ethics and Action*. London: Routledge and Kegan Paul.
Wolterstorff, N. (1980), *Works and Worlds of Art*. Oxford: Clarendon Press.
Wood, M. (2005), *Literature and the Taste of Knowledge*. Cambridge: Cambridge University Press.
Woolf, V. ([1924] 1996), 'Mr Bennett and Mrs Brown', in M. J. Hoffman and P. D. Murphy (eds), *Essentials of the Theory of Fiction*, 24–39. Durham: Duke University Press.
Woolf, V. ([1925] 2008), 'Modern Fiction', in Woolf, *Selected Essays*, ed. D. Bradshaw, 6–12. Oxford: Oxford University Press.
Woolf, V. (1978), *The Diary of Virginia Woolf, Volume II: 1920–1923*, ed. A. O. Bell. London: The Hogarth Press.
von Wright, G. H. (2001), *Mitt liv som jag minns det* ["My Life as I Remember it"]. Stockholm: Söderström.
Ylikoski, P. (2009), 'The Illusion of Depth of Understanding in Science', in H. W. de Regt, S. Leonelli and K. Eigner (eds), *Scientific Understanding*, 100–19. Pittsburgh: University of Pittsburgh Press.
Zagzebski, L. (2001), 'Recovering Understanding', in M. Steup (ed.), *Knowledge Truth, and Duty: Essays on Epistemic Justification, Responsibility, and Virtue*, 235–51. Oxford: Oxford University Press.
Zagzebski, L. (2009), *On Epistemology*. Belmont: Wadsworth.
Zahavi, D. (2007), 'Self and Other: The Limits of Narrative Understanding', in D. D. Hutto (ed.), *Narrative and Understanding Persons*, 179–201. Cambridge: Cambridge University Press.
Zamir, T. (2007), *Double Vision: Moral Vision and Shakespearean Drama*. Princeton: Princeton University Press.
Zamir, T. (2019), *Just Literature: Philosophical Criticism and Justice*. New York: Routledge.
Zunshine, L. (2006), *Why We Read Fiction: Theory of Mind and the Novel*. Columbus: Ohio State University Press.

Index

Alber, J.   73, 100–1
Anderson, L.   67

Bruner, J.   42, 72

Camus, A.   79–80
Carrol, N.   71–2, 103, 105
cognition, *see also* understanding
   and confusion   75–6, 77–80,
      81–3, 83–5
   definition of   5–8, 68–70, 76–7
   as knowledge   59–60
cognitive narratology   61,
      67, 73, 100–1
cognitivism
   definition of   7, 86
   objectivist and
      relational   112–16
Cooper, D.   53, 115
Currie, G.   14–15, 17, 35–6, 91–2,
      97, 99–100, 110

Davis, C.   79–80
Dostoyevsky, F.   35, 104, 106,
      109, 111, 118

Eco, U.   21, 31–2
Elgin, C. Z.   51–2, 116
evidence, *see* methods

Fludernik, M.   61, 64, 73, 98–9

Goldie, P.   55–6
Goodman, N.   47, 87

Hakemulder, F.   2, 96
Harrison, B.   6, 77

Herman, D.   60, 61–2

imagination
   and art   18, 19–21, 24–6,
      28, 31
   as an attitude and an
      activity   17, 26
   and fantasy   21–4
   and genre   27–31
   as immersion   15–16
   modes of   13–15, 16–17
   and reflection   33–9
Ingarden, R.   19–20
interpretation
   literary   19–21, 26, 28, 35, 36,
      61, 65, 75, 80, 90–1, 92, 98,
      100–1, 103, 105, 113
   and use   31–2
Iser, W.   15–16, 20

John, E.   77–8, 84, 106

Kidd, D. C. and E. Castano   93–5
Kivy, P.   38–9
knowledge, *see* cognition

Lamarque, P.   23–4, 25, 36–7, 43,
      46–8, 49, 65–6, 67–8,
      83–4, 103, 115

methods
   empirical psychology   92–101
   and justification   90–1
   introspection   90–2
   literary reception
      study   105–12
   metacriticism   102–5

narrative
    and genre 46–9
    and knowledge 43–6, 49–50
    understanding 50–3
Novitz, D. 71, 72, 78
Nussbaum, M. 74

Palmer, A. 60, 61
Panero, M. 97, 98
Posner, R. 75–6, 114–15

Ricœur, P. 50, 55

Schopenhauer, A. 15, 16

theory of mind 61, 64, 65–6, 67

understanding
    the concept of 51–2, 70
    and literature 54–7, 71–2, 85–8
    and misunderstanding 64–5, 74, 109–10

Walton, K. 14–15, 22–3, 25, 35–6
Woolf, V. 62–4, 66–7, 90
Wright, G. H. von 109, 111, 118

Zagzebski, L. 51, 108
Zamir, T. 6, 55

www.ingramcontent.com/pod-product-compliance
Lightning Source LLC
Chambersburg PA
CBHW070640300426
44111CB00013B/2191